Links of Healing

The Chains That Built Me

Peggy Warner Ayers

with

Mary Parkin

ISBN-13: 978-1497353626
ISBN-10: 1497353629

Dedication

To my selfless parents, priceless husband,
precious children, and irreplaceable friends and family.
But most of all my words are for my Master Healer,
Christ, because without Him I have no story.

Contents

To protect the rights and identities
of certain individuals, some names
have been changed.

I Believe...

As a member of the Church of Jesus Christ of Latter-day Saints who has a testimony of the pre-existence—where all of God's children lived with Him before we came to this earth—I believe I agreed to my personal mortal journey, and to the trials I would come here to face. This solid conviction did not cement in my heart, however, until about five years ago when I made the choice to confront and forgive the person who, for several years, inflicted traumatizing abuse.

From the ages of five to ten, I was molested by my pediatrician. For the next thirty-five years of my life I became a fireball of backlash, bitterness, and resentment. On the surface I was bubbly, lighthearted, and maybe a bit reckless, but inside I was a churning crucible of turmoil. I felt entitled to my anger. Like many who suffer tragedy, I shook my fist at God, cursing the path He, I felt, put me on. I hated all forms of control from school principals to overpowering coaches. But most of all, I hated myself. I felt worthless. Because I was a child, I did not understand what had been taken from me, only that it was important and that without it I was a light extinguished.

When I was seventeen, I received a special blessing from an ordained member of my church called a Patriarch. My Patriarchal

Blessing, he said, would guide me through life's uncertain terrain, warn me of hazards, enlighten me with potential blessings, and serve as a caveat for improper choices. One paragraph in the blessing seemed so painfully specific that for years whenever I reread my transcribed copy I would skip over it, discarding the sacred words. It said how my greatness will be measured by how well I accepted the trials and tests and happenings in my life that seemed unfair and undeserved; that they were for edification and growth which was divinely customized to give me the experiences I was foreordained to receive; and that the times of my greatest trials would also be the times of my greatest growth. I was assured that the Lord Jesus Christ would be close to me in my many hours of need, guiding and directing me on the path of truth and righteousness. Lastly, the blessing said that I would never be alone, and that I would feel the Lord's closeness in times of discouragement and despair.

Although the promise of divine comfort brought peace to my soul, the part about my trials being designed for me struck me like a knife in the chest. How could I have accepted my path of abuse, teenage rebellion, and later the inability to bear my own children? Again and again I read those words, which I know came from God's mind to the Patriarch's mouth, and I ached because they meant He knew my pain yet still allowed me to walk this thorny path. How could a loving Heavenly Father watch his daughter live through such horror? I loved my Heavenly Father, but I couldn't accept that my trials were for my personal growth. For years, I played the victim of a life I was cursed to tread.

Then one day, nearly two decades later, a still, small voice inside my heart posed *this* question to me: "Peggy," it beckoned, "what if *you* agreed to your trials?"

I felt like a patient in an optometrist's chair. The Lord was my spiritual physician, clicking through lenses and asking me which was clearer: lens one or lens two? Did my vision improve when I blinded myself to the answers already given me in a Lord's blessing? When I finally accepted the truth of my trial, I began to find strength in the possibility that in the pre-Earth life—when I knew God personally and loved Him unconditionally—*He* believed in *me* with so much faith as to ask me to journey a bitter course. When I said yes, I knew I would not be a helpless and vulnerable victim, but I would have the strength of giants behind my walls of character.

I believe I was called to life's mission of experiencing sexual abuse as a child and the effects of the trauma. I believe this without a shadow of a doubt. My only regret is keeping this truth tucked away for so long. I know that God does not create abusers to prey upon us; rather, He possesses the foreknowledge and the wisdom to turn a victim into a victory. In the end, the prize of that victory is a joy beyond measure only heavenly eyes can comprehend.

Each of us is on a journey of self-discovery. If we accept help from above, our lives will unfurl more gloriously than any fairytale we could read about. Together with the Savior Jesus Christ and His atonement, we can find joy in our journeys, no matter what obstacles challenge us. This is my hope and my reason for letting go of the dark and embracing the light. I invite you, dear reader, to embrace the light, too. By sharing my story with you, I pray that hope will abound, faith increase, and testimonies strengthen.

Opposition as a Child

"And I said unto him: I know that he loveth his children;
nevertheless, I do not know the meaning of all things."
~Alma 36:3

My darling friend Julie Tate once used the term "front loaded" to describe how, for some children, life's difficulties come at the beginning of their lives instead of during their teenage or even adult years. I was one of those children. For the most part I had a normal, pleasant childhood. I grew up in a safe neighborhood and was raised by goodly parents and loving siblings. I had friends, creative spaces to play, and double the opportunities my siblings had because I was the youngest and came at the tail end of Dad's career. I would spend hours outside with my friends, jumping on the trampoline in my backyard, building forts out of the wind-blown trees which had fallen down one fall, and splitting into teams to play various games like "Search" (a team version of Hide-and-Go-Seek) and "Capture the Flag." We clawed through storm drains pretending we were adventurers, and sledded down the snow-painted hills of the nearby golf course.

Alecia Thompson, Ashley Brooks, Barbara Flynn, and Sarah Scalley were some of my dearest partners in crime. As we practiced violin and shoveled walks, making mounds into snow caves, our friendships were being constructed on solid blocks of humor, love, and a zest to dance and do gymnastics till our bodies fell to the ground. Their homes were my second, third, and fourth homes. I loved their parents and siblings like my own.

My mom was such an asset to our community that she was gone many nights a week, serving the single mothers or speaking at a Lambda Delta (an LDS college sorority) event. "She is more precious than rubies" (Proverbs 3:15) could not describe her better. She inherited a ruby ring that she has worn my whole life, symbolizing that her worth is beyond the price of gems.

Nancy, my second oldest sister, would put me to bed some nights with her tender, soft touch. She would take off her necklace and ever so gently drape it across my face to help me fall asleep. There was an age span of 19 years between my oldest sibling Wendy and I. She was a beautiful mentor along with Nancy, but because she married when I was only three, I did not get to know her as closely until years later. I was blessed to visit her and my other siblings when they married, and as I got older I gained younger siblings as nieces and nephews. Wendy's son Weston—my little buddy—was only five years younger than me. Abbey, his little sister, was a curious head of sweet curls whom I adored babysitting for hours on end later in my life.

I was kind of a floater. I loved action, sports, and just simply being with people. I would be the first to want to go on an adventure even if it was as simple as going to 7-Eleven. My brother Dave and his wife Pam's house was the place I could really let down my hair, though. I played for hours with their daughter Heidi who was only six years younger than me.

I also loved my alone time. I loved to draw with crisp, brand new crayons or pull out my white roller skates—even if it meant risking a skinned knee or two. Mom was my safe place to land. Her smell, touch, and comforting arms embraced me tirelessly, as I was an active child and curious as a cat. If I thought of Heaven, her arms were the clouds to lift me there. The love I had for her was bottomless. She had a knack for feeling my pain before I did, anticipating a need before the words could come out. Her quest for children was on going, even after suffering the loss of my second oldest sister (also named Heidi), who was born premature at seven months, passing away four days later. (She would have been 17 years older than me.) Mom had me at age 44, and had yet another miscarriage after that. I was her last shot at holding an infant in her arms.

I was the only one Dad was able to witness being born; he flew home early from a business trip. I think this bonded us from the start. He, too, was a piece of heaven. In the summer, my dad and I would walk those same hills I slid down with my friends, hand-in-hand, saying prayers for the day and chasing after our Alaskan malamute, Jane, as she harassed the porcupines. (She would occasionally come back with quills stuck in her nose.) I knew God was tender from a young age because my parents both reflected His kindness in their eyes.

I was blessed with three older brothers: Dave, Gill, and Ned. They were my knights in shining armor, and I lived to be near them. Many days I had wished I were a younger brother so they would accept me more, but in the end I kept up with all of their activities pretty well. We bonded while playing night games on our front lawn with the neighborhood kids. We were kind of the pit stop for group-gathering Sunday nights. Good, solid families in our neighborhood like The Halls, Cowleys, and Christensens surrounded us like a buffer of a "Beaver Cleaver" girth, reining us all in if we stayed out too late.

Looking back, you would have thought Peggy really did have it all. Life was a fairytale. But as with most fairytales, there needs to be opposition in order to appreciate the sweetness of the story. My story starts at the age of five.

I heard Mom calling, but I didn't answer. It wasn't her tone of voice—rushed for time—that made me afraid, but what it meant when she said the words, "It's time to go to the doctor." I ran to the laundry room, where I hid behind the dusty washing machine like a stowaway. I didn't have words for my fear, just a face and a certain touch I didn't like. The word "molest" hadn't been introduced on my list of kindergarten vocabulary words. All I could muster up to say was, "I don't want to go to him!"

Using my child logic, I reasoned that if I couldn't see Mom, she couldn't see me. "Peggy, we'll be late," she said. She slung her purse over her shoulder and dusted off my red polyester pants, now coated with lint. Mom took my hand and guided me down the hall to the garage. It was not unusual for her to have to assist me along to get to places, as I was usually in my own world daydreaming. But this was a different, more passionate resistance. Escape routes crowded my mind. I could slip away and beeline it back down the hallway; I could race upstairs to my bedroom and hide in the closet. But like all the times before, Mom would find me. She didn't understand why I fought so hard as she buckled me into our green station wagon. All five of her living children disliked going to the doctor, so she assumed I wasn't much different.

My chest tightened as the car revved, driving me into a recurring nightmare. My friends waved to me from their front lawns; I willed my hand to wave back, but it was holding fast to the seatbelt harnessing me in. I was trapped, and I would feel trapped for many years to come.

We turned onto 21st South and the scenery morphed into a cityscape with grocery stores and a shopping mall. Sugar House Park was aglow with sunlight pouring down fertile hills. My heart yearned for our journey to end here—or the ice skating rink down the street. I disliked the cold, but I was willing to trade one discomfort for another.

By the end of the drive, I had curled myself into the fetal position. Mom carried me up the steps to a door with chipping paint. In that moment, I resented her almost as much as I resented my pediatrician, simply because I felt trapped in my emotions. I was doing everything I could to express my fears, but it was like I was caught behind a wall of glass and she couldn't hear me. Prone to tantrums, I found that resisting and crying louder only made my pain harder to hear. Mom had not an ounce of darkness in her and so it didn't even cross her mind that she was leading me into a snake pit of pythons, regardless of my resisting.

The receptionist's desk seemed uncommonly high, towering over me as if to disguise secrets of malpractice. The woman behind it was kind yet oblivious as she instructed us to have a seat on the chairs shoved against the coffee-brown and pickle-green papered walls. My heart felt like a thousand pounds of pressure. I wasn't able to convey what was festering in me because of my limited understanding of what I felt was real. Why could no one else see it but me?

My stomach tumbled. As I gnawed my fingernails to nubs, Mom sat contently, thumbing through a children's magazine. She was brimming with confidence for this doctor, who was an old schoolmate of hers. They ran in the same circles, played together and laughed together. Across the years he had groomed my parents well, never giving them reason to doubt him.

A nurse dressed in white with a little starched hat tilted on her head came into the waiting room, and I knew I was the next patient on her list. Like with mom, I don't think any of the nurses or staff had a clue what was happening beyond the waiting room. They were innocent bystanders unknowingly helping camouflage their employer's sick addiction.

"Peggy?" she said, looking at me fondly. I've never liked my name, even though I inherited it from my grandmother Erma Oles Marler Mortensen, who liked to be called Peggy (which was her stage name). When I was young, a few boys in my grade thought it was funny to call me "Piggy Peggy," but that's not why I hated it. I hated it because of how foreboding it sounded paired with the dry scrape of the nurse's finger scrolling down her manila folder. When she said my name it meant that I was the doctor's next victim.

Immediately, I switched into survival mode, turning myself off like a spider does to survive fumigation. It was all I could do as the nurse led Mom and me down a short hallway and into the examination room, which was too bright for my eyes and had a sterile smell that burned my nose. The walls seemed to loom over me like nightmarish shadows at dusk.

Waiting for the doctor to enter almost felt worse than what he would do to me. It made knots of my nerves, and my little body quivered with anxiety. I felt like a ragdoll, a plaything trapped in a toy box.

The door opened and Dr. Strover came towards me, his eyes beating behind dark, cat-eyed glasses. He was shorter than the average man, and a bit plump. He pushed a hand through his creepy, wavy black hair as he looked over my patient's file. I wonder now what reasons my medical records gave him to violate me. Taking a seat on his swivel chair, he said, "Let's check the ears," and scooted close.

The otoscope was large and uncomfortable as he shoved it into my right ear, then left, surveying the inside for an abundance of yellow wax. You'd think he'd struck gold the way he grinned, pulling an ear pick from his lab coat. The icy, hooked metal flashed balefully as it dug around, painfully extracting flakes of wax. I cringed, but I didn't cry. I told myself to be brave because this wasn't even the worse part of the "check-up."

He'd told my mother that little girls tended to "close up" down there and needed attention. Because he was a professional with a degree from a semi-prestigious medical school framed on his wall, she never questioned him. In the mid-70s you just didn't. If he had been anything but a doctor, Mom confessed later, it would have been so easy to stop it. That's all I wanted, to stop it. Yet his deceit was buried under years of grooming my parents for trust, and hidden under a believable medical condition.

When the abuse started, I checked out. My emotions launched into the atmosphere in order to protect my mental state. I like to believe that God removed my spirit from my body for a while. He could have possibly taken me into His arms and held me, reminding me that there is another type of touch besides a selfish one.

Leaving the doctor's office was like finding an oasis in the desert, except now I felt unalterably blemished as if my self-image had become diseased. This precious gift from God which was reserved for the sacred bonds of marriage had now been twisted, the knots so gnarled it would take the rest of my life to unravel them. Trust had been tainted by deception and fear.

From the moment it started, the abuse consumed my every thought. It leaked into my dreams. Instead of imagining recipes for mud pies or playing carelessly with my friends, I was devising ideas of other ways I could be examined so that the doctor wouldn't have to touch me. It may sound twisted, but to my five-year-old brain, it was logical. I didn't have the power to stop going to him, and I couldn't adequately express to my parents what I was feeling.

When others thought I was daydreaming or off in my own world, I was really wondering if what was happening to me was really what it was. No one had ever explained sexual abuse to me, so all I knew to verbalize was that I hated his touch. I started to question if what I felt was really off from reality, yet my inner light knew it was wrong and started to create ways around facing the truth. To keep quiet and cope internally felt safer than risking being ignored for my feelings. The battle was lost before I entered his exam room.

ℭ

When I was little I liked to sign all notes I wrote with the phrase "that's true" right before my name. Deep down, my little soul was searching for the truth and cried out for it in any way possible. Yet the truth would not be discovered until after many years of heartache and inner turmoil. I longed for some way to release the heartache of this horrible torture I was subjected to during my yearly checkups (and more often, when my ears ached), but I didn't know how to soundly describe this desire to those around me.

Pain like this requires a balm, but my five-year-old self had no idea what kind of help I needed. I turned to one of the humblest of coping mechanisms: raising rabbits. Somehow, thinking about my next rabbit took me into a brighter world. I would scroll through the newspaper, searching for ads for dwarf bunnies. My parents, although good sports, weren't that excited about anymore pets crowding our house, but I was usually able to convince them how much I needed this through a major tantrum.

One day my sweet dad drove me miles to see the rabbits I'd found in the paper. We came home with two. Salt, a male, was white like snow; and pepper, a multi-colored female, was his companion. Soon, they were producing litter after litter of little fuzz-balls like themselves. I was always drawn to the runt of each litter. Being the youngest child at home, I could easily relate. I did everything I could to make sure that one-inch miracle got to the nursing nest or latched onto its mother for a good milking at least twice a day. I saw its worth, even when I couldn't see my own. Saving the runt seemed to parallel my own position in the family. At times I felt defective and helpless, unable to express my pain properly to everyone older than me.

Mom would wake me up at 5:30 in the morning to help feed the newborns before school. Eyes shut tight, their velvety bodies huddled close to their mother as they sucked. These moments captured in the wee hours of the morning held precious exchanges of nurturing. I was never judged or hurt by these small animals, and nurturing them distracted me from painful memories and thoughts of worthlessness. To these bunnies, I was worth everything. They needed my care to keep them alive. As I grew older, my coping mechanisms evolved, pushing my pain deeper into my subconscious. Yet my inner turmoil always seemed to find a way of leaking onto the surface. I felt trapped in binding chains, with no way out.

Left: me and my doll Suzanne
Bottom: my childhood home

Top left: Me, age 3, playing in the mud with no idea what was coming
Top right: Age 5, when the abuse started

Link 2:

Furnace of Affliction

"For, behold, I have refined thee,
I have chosen thee in the furnace of affliction."
~1 Nephi 20:10

A battle forged in my little body so deep I would not understand why or how until much later in life, when it all came to a head. For the most part, adults can usually communicate their distress, but as an adolescent I couldn't understand why I was being taken to a man who was torturing me. I wanted my voice to be heard, but more than that I wanted peace. Much like the rabbits, toys and other material things had a way of calming my inner storm.

Almost every little girl innately has it in her to love a doll of some sorts, and mine was named Suzanne. She was magical. On Christmas morning my mom played her famous tune on the piano and all the siblings marched around the flocked tree, laced with gorgeous pink ornaments and white lights. The rule was that we could not sit next to our presents until the song stopped. As soon as the final notes rang out I ran over to the life-size doll and cuddled her close to me. She felt as real as my young nieces and nephew, whom I adored.

Suzanne's hands were curled and humanlike. She had curly auburn hair and chocolate eyes that closed when you put her down. I'd swaddle her in a pale yellow quilt made by my sister-in-law, Pam, and tuck her into a basinet my parents had used for me. When the dark hours of the day approached, I checked on her frequently, quickly pulling her onto my bed to make sure she was okay. When I needed to do chores or wanted to play with my stuffed monkey, Buttons, for a while, I bundled Suzanne up in her quilt, fed her a bottle, and tucked her into the basinet. She always knew she was my top priority; whenever she cried I would be by her side in an instant like any good mother.

When her left eye started to malfunction, so did I. I broke down into a typhoon-sized tantrum and begged Mom to fix it. Thankfully, she pulled out a phone book and flipped through the yellow pages for a doll doctor. Taking Suzanne to that saintly woman was the equivalent of Mom hearing my cry for help. If I could not be fixed, at least Suzanne could.

My want for certain things my parents told me I did not need often led to severe tantrums. I remember seeing a specialized yoyo being advertised on TV and thinking, *I have got to have this no matter what!* That yoyo "walking the dog" across the vibrant screen became my central focus of survival. I petitioned my parents to buy it for me, as I literally thought my world would come to an end if I didn't get it.

I shut myself up in my bedroom and cried for hours until they finally bought it for me. I honestly believed that yoyo would save my fragile life. As absurd as it sounds, for that brief moment of holding it, my war for peace felt subdued, taking my mind off of the restlessness in my body.

Trying the best she could, Mom would eventually give in and buy the toys I wanted. Her heart ached to understand why nothing seemed to satisfy her daughter.

Other times we'd be in the checkout line at the store, and I would fixate on a cheap toy or candy bar, wailing terribly and bargaining with my parents. Other customers would judge and stare. My parents were always so loving and generous; they truly didn't know what was wrong with me. I was trying to fill a black hole with material objects, yet it was never enough. The sensation of something new would wear off as quickly as I opened the package, and the unquenchable void of darkness would envelope my quickly fading self-image.

My parents interpreted my tantrums as red flags, proving I needed correction because nothing else seemed to link to my outbursts. Who was Peggy becoming if not an undisciplined child who raged when she didn't get her way? Back then, at least in our small circumference, it seemed like there were no underlying causes to certain behaviors, just the problematic attitude of a child who needed to be evaluated, medicated, and corrected. So for the second year of my education I was transferred to a private Christian school called Carden Memorial, which was heavy on manners, rules, and etiquette. Students were required to stand when adults came into the room. We wore itchy polyester uniforms in patriotic colors and checkered patterns. Our white pixy collars had to be smooth and straight, and our socks and shoes had to be just right. The soft cotton sweater with the school's emblem stitched to the chest pocket felt like a prisoner's uniform. This school became my new sterile exam room, and the teachers and administration were the wardens keeping me trapped for eight hours a day. Strictness resembled control, which triggered a feeling of losing my freedom reflected in past emotions from the doctor's office. (At this time, however, I would not consciously make this connection.)

There was a uniquely designed fence stretching through the neighborhood where the school was located, surrounding the last house as cars rounded the carpool lane. I imagined climbing the chain-link section encasing the playground and following the wood section as it stretched towards home. Being so young, I figured if I could follow other landmarks such as this one I could find my way home alone. At recess this daydream filled my mind; that fence seemed like my road to freedom and safety.

I missed my mom with a ripening intensity that consumed my every thought. I pleaded with her not to leave me, and even solicited the principal to allow her to become a teacher there. When I understood it was impossible for her to be with me all the time, I felt abandoned and confused. Just like an infant crying out because she's unable to say *I want a bottle,* I did everything I could to break through the confines of the prison. I knew my mom's tangible closeness felt like my only safe place, but I couldn't comprehend why I didn't feel safe at school or elsewhere. The doctor's office had become the grimy lens I saw through, and I was still emotionally trapped in his exam room, yet I wouldn't recognize it for decades to come.

As the winters passed into my later elementary years, my teachers quickly learned to keep me separated from my friends Alecia, Ashley, and Barbara, because we'd chatter and laugh during lectures. But even on opposite sides of the room, we had our way of communicating with each other through our facial expressions. Our favorite was the "Mr. Furley," which was based off a character in the sitcom *Three's Company.*

Once, after we had caused a big ruckus with our flippant laughter, an announcement came over the PA system for all orchestra members to report to the outside classroom for practice. Alecia and I stood up to go and our teacher looked at us, or at least at *me,* as if to make a snide remark like, "I can't believe you'd ever be involved in orchestra...." It was as if she was implying I was a menace to society, when really I was just trying to have a little fun.

I remember spending one afternoon in the library, intensely studying for my math class. I was a hard worker most of the time; my homework got turned in and my desk was meticulously organized— almost to the point of being O.C.D. Principal Johns paced between the rows of students, peering over shoulders to see what they we working on and if we needed any help. When he reached me, he bent low and said, "Peggy, you ought not to extend yourself too high in math, as it is not your best subject."

Honestly, I'm sure he meant well, but my self-worth was already as low as it could be, and now I was picking up every scrap of evidence I could to prove how repulsive and worthless I was. It didn't seem to matter how hard I worked, or how straight my feather berets hung against my curly chestnut hair, all anyone could ever see was my behavior, not the brittle foundation of my self-worth crumbling with each negative remark.

My perspective was shifting. If no one was going to see the good in me, then I was going to water those parts of me and my behavior that kept surfacing. I was going to laugh as loud as I could and at all costs. I resented nearly all forms of authority. The tighter they squeezed, the harder I resisted, landing me in the principal's office more than once over the seven years I attended Carden. I was a misfit who quite possibly was only allowed back each year for the mere fact that my parents were contributing donors to the private school's money fund (though that's just speculation on my part). School felt like invisible shackles keeping me from experiencing the true freedom I so longed to find.

One of the few people who seemed to see past the behavior into the pain in my heart was my sister-in-law Pam, who was married to my oldest brother Dave. Pam knew how to just let me be *me* without any rules or conditions. If I wanted to eat cookie dough and play Miss Pac Man for a good two hours, she let me. She even let me pick the cherries off her tree in her backyard. She knew how to simply let me be myself, with no expectations.

What made me love Pam more than anything was that she believed every word I said about my pediatrician. She broke down the delusion I had that I was alone and made me feel safe. She did her best to convince my parents that what was happening to me was painful and real, but because of their close relationship with Dr. Strover and his sneakiness to hide it under a medical condition, the visits persisted for five long years.

And then one day, a miracle happened.

I remember the day like it was an hour ago. It was afternoon. The sun shot gold beams through Pam and Dave's kitchen window. I sat at their round metal table with their daughter Heidi, eating cookie dough right off a wooden spoon, when Pam rushed in through the back door. She stopped in front of me and sighed, the biggest smile on her face.

"Peggy, I have the best news!" she said.

"What?" I asked.

She took a relieved breath. "You will never have to see Dr. Strover again."

I felt a tangible cloud of heavy darkness lift from my shoulders in that moment. I could barely believe it was true. And yet it was absolutely true. Dr. Strover had been caught with inappropriate photos of young children and had also been accused of exposing himself to two young girls in downtown Salt Lake. His medical license was revoked. I was never going to see his sick, twisted expression again.

Looking back at age ten, I wondered why my parents weren't the first to tell me. Was it too hard? I had longed for this for the past five years of my life, but the conversation was brushed over like before. Even though I was ecstatic Dr. Strover's medical practice had been closed down, not being acknowledged by my parents made me feel like they were sweeping the secret of my abuse under a rug. It was as if they were thinking: *Maybe this happened to someone else's child, but not to ours.*

Regardless of who shared the news with me, for this brief moment in time it felt like a bitter cup had passed from my lips. A chink lifted in my shackled heart, temporally freeing me, even though the image of my enemy retreating was but a mirage.

Weston, Me, Heidi, and Mom

Me (left), Alecia
Thompson
(back), and
Ashley Brooks
(right)

Starting to feel
trapped,
kindergarten

Age 10, with my
dad at Ned's
graduation from
junior high

Link 3:

Friction and Resentment

"For it must needs be, that there is an opposition in all things. If not so...righteousness could not be brought to pass, neither wickedness, neither holiness nor misery, neither good nor bad."

~2 Nephi 2:11

The summer of fifth grade proved to expose more than awkward puberty. I along with several other youth from my neighborhood took a computer class in downtown Salt Lake City, right off of South Temple by the Lion's Club. We were all bummed because it was summer and our parents were making us take a several week course. Only the carpool proved fun as we pressed our faces against the car windows, making silly faces at other drivers and giggling till our sides hurt.

As soon as we entered the classroom, which looked more like a drab business office, I was on edge. A man was teaching the course. Mr. Keys was dry and strict, and I immediately felt this power struggle between us. Throughout the class I would call out smug remarks, bored out of my mind and hating being cooped indoors when I should have been outside playing in the grass with the bugs and my friends.

"That's enough, Peggy," he reprimanded me, but I ignored him. Something in me screamed to rebel on every level. I think unknowingly I got off on irritating him because it meant he couldn't control or use me like Dr. Strover had. Mr. Keys presented a release valve that I could pull to expel a good portion of my pent-up anger. It had been a year since Pam told me I didn't have to see my pediatrician anymore, and my psyche was giving me permission to vent in any way I could, regardless of the consequences. Unfortunately, there are always consequences.

Over a period of several weeks I seemed to get to know the hallway better than the keyboard, as I was sent out to think about my sharp tongue more often than not. A spark of rebellion had been lit and getting scolded only fueled me to rebel on new levels. If I was not going to be teacher's pet, I would be the voice of all those in the class whose tongues were also tied. My reputation was already blemished, so to cry out for the lost ones became my mantra regardless of the consequences. I would fight not only *my* battles, but also the battles for others who felt misunderstood as I did. If I couldn't be heard for my inner conflict I would find a way to show it through body language instead.

One autumn afternoon as a sixth grader back at Carden, I was staring out a classroom window, watching a cyclone of leaves wrestle with the air and dreaming of diving into the massive piles in my own front yard (which my family would most likely have spent hours raking after school). Just then a voice sounded over the intercom: *Will Peggy Warner please come to the office with all of her belongings? She's being checked out.*

Excited, I put away my eraser, which I had meticulously rubbed clean of smudge marks from all the day's mistakes, packed up all my school gear, and hurried to the office. Thoughts flurried through my mind about the unexpected checkout. *What's the occasion?* I wondered.

As I raced up the ramp to the office, I saw Mom. *Yes!* I thought. *She's here to break me out of Alcatraz!* I was thrilled to have my boredom appeased, but the thrill wouldn't last long.

We pulled into the University of Utah visitor's parking lot, and then walked over to the Social and Behavioral Sciences Building, where I met with a behavioral psychologist. He asked me a string of random questions that seemed so silly to me. I'd give him quick, equally random replies just to get the whole thing over with. But we were just getting started. In addition to the questions, I had to take a series of strange tests. For one of them, I was put in a room all alone with a pile of blocks in front of me, which I had to arrange in a certain fashion.

On the way back to the car, Mom handed me a Snickers bar, attempting to soften the punch of that uncomfortable experience. Chocolate was our choice of home remedies; most of us had a sweet tooth.

The tests extended over many years, with a variety of psychologists, and each time I felt more like a lab rat. Every time I heard my name being called over the school PA system, my body would go numb. I labeled myself as "defective," because that's how I felt meeting with a psychologist and knowing my family was being studied for mental illness. We had such a long history of bipolar, depression, and anxiety disorders that any sign of malfunction directed us straight to the Petri dish for observation. I am not exactly sure what conclusions they came to concerning me, but it seemed to spark their interest for yearly tests.

No one ever brought up the abuse, only my poor behavior. Because my family never brought it out into the open or pressed charges, I got this strange idea that maybe I was making it into a bigger deal than it was. Deep within I knew what the doctor had done was wrong and unlawful, but because it was a young girl's word pitted against a medical professional's convincing diagnosis and treatment, I just didn't have the support I needed (though he had been caught doing other misdeeds). So keeping it quiet—pushing it to the background—felt safer than trying to prove a point I didn't comprehend on much of any level.

Eventually as a preteen, I started to blindly accept textbook theories of me having anxiety and depression. A history of mental illness surged through my family's veins, so I guess it made sense. Over time, I fell prey to the belief that all I needed to do to get better was to submit to a certain diagnosis and dutifully take the prescribed medications. Yet in reality, all those tests and drugs and therapy sessions were just masking the root of the problem.

A new link of being tied to a family genetic disorder now seemed to trump the only good reason of hating my abuser. I felt like Rapunzel under a mental disorder, locked up in a tower for my unwanted behavior. Subconsciously, I felt like I was sentenced to a life of toil and limitations. I felt like I needed to accept the fact that this was as good as it was going to get, and that there was no other reason than this for my pain. I was not being cruel to myself; I merely lacked the understanding of what the abuse had really done to my psyche. Like the rest of my family, this was the only way I knew how to cope, regardless of my resentment at the time. I played the victim, mad at the world—mad at my family's diagnosis—just mad!

CR

I thought it odd when junior high rolled around and my friends Alecia, Ashley, and Barbara were not as eager to graduate from the prison-like feel of Carden as I was. I would listen to them reminisce over treasured memories, and I would scrunch up my forehead wondering what they had experienced that I missed. *Did we even go to the same school?* Was my soul so twisted that I saw through warped eyes? The whole world felt like a perpetrator, and I was its favorite victim. Suddenly, I felt estranged from my best friends because of my tainted viewpoint of life. When I looked in the mirror, I saw myself as a rebellious young girl who not only was rejected by life, but was dirty for somehow believing I attracted the abuse. Were there others, or was I the only girl the doctor had touched wrongly? Maybe I was worthless, and that is what drew him in. The more pieces my mind tried to force into the puzzle, the more I longed to see what my friends saw, feel what they felt. I envied their carefree, unblemished view of childhood.

This isn't to say I didn't have a few fond memories of my time at Carden. I often think back to my time spent with Mrs. Johns, the principal's strict yet on rare occasions gentle wife, who would gather a few of us children under her wings like chicks. She'd usher us into a little room that felt like a secret hideaway, and in soft tones read to us from *The Tales of Benjamin Bunny*. Those moments were magical, even when my heart was in shackles.

I entered the halls of Hillside Jr. High absolutely boy crazy. In my journal I made a list of ten boys whom I liked, though who didn't necessarily like me back. I then made it clear that I only liked four seriously, though. I felt this wave of opportunity to find my self-esteem. If at least one of these boys liked me, then maybe I'd be worth something. The sad thing is how easily opportunity turned into obsession. Even in grade school, I couldn't play a game of flag football without hoping the match turned into a tackle, so that cute Johnny Lineman would accidentally bump into me, giving me a chance to gaze into those gorgeous brown eyes. A part in me had been unlocked early in that sick physician's room even if I had hated every minute of it. I didn't understand how to put it back into its rightful cage.

My name, for the most part, was known all over the school with the attached stigma that I liked a new boy every week. "Just once," I told my mother, "I would love people to find out how many boys I insisted 'move on' to! But those things don't seem to matter to a vindictive crowd."

I was once at a school dance with a boy whom I really liked, and during our slow dance seven other boys asked to cut in. I felt like a rag doll being thrown around while the whole school watched. I was so confused. I thought these boys were genuinely trying to befriend me, but it turned out I was just a subject of bullying and ridicule. Deeply embarrassed, I wondered what was wrong with me. A fog horn went off, blaring a new ultimatum: I was not going to be used. I would be the user.

Some of the girls at school were hostile towards me because they thought I was stealing their boyfriends. I unknowingly crossed into their territories when their boyfriends started showing interest in me. My heart was broken just as many times as theirs, yet I seemed to be the one to blame, not the boy's calling me.

One morning, I woke up to some not so nice things spelled out on my front lawn with shaving cream. My sweet brothers Gill and Ned rushed outside and cleaned up the mess before our parents could see. I was crushed! I couldn't understand why this was happening—especially since the vandal was the former girlfriend of my crush who had broken up with me to get back together with her. Was losing the guy I really liked not hurtful enough?

My heart wasn't only breaking over the boy I shared my first kiss with, but also over these friends whom I weaved bracelets with at Brighten Girls Camp. Drawing a barrier across my own front lawn was like a warning to stay off other girls' property. Once again, I felt I was being misunderstood, backed into a corner by people misinterpreting my actions. I simply wanted to be loved and accepted, just like they did. My self-esteem was already so low, but being bullied compounded the truth that I was used-up and no good. This war between what my parents had taught me—that I am a special daughter of God—and my feelings of worthlessness extinguished what flicker of light still burned within me. And now there was a new worry in my life: if I couldn't trust girls as well as boys, what shell of defense could I use to keep danger at bay? My trust became almost nonexistent.

I hardly mentioned the abuse or my pain to any of my friends. If my parents didn't acknowledge the act, I got it in my head that my friends probably wouldn't either. I still felt unsure of all the details of what truly happened, and that I was simply a disturbed girl only valuable to the world of psychology and medical studies for future science. It was like I had bought a time-share in "Victimville" and the benefit package was a pass to vent all my aggression and unwanted feelings on my surroundings.

I remember a rare time during my freshman year at Highland High School when a good friend and I were in her kitchen, discussing what I had been through, and her mom out of the blue piped up and said, "I took Angie to him once, but he gave me the creeps! So I never took her back." My heart ached as I thought, *Here is a mom who saw it right off and never went back, so what is wrong with me?* Was I that worthless that I was not enough to save? Was I so overlooked that my parents didn't feel I was worthy to fight for? Or was I that inarticulate that what I had to say fell on deaf ears? I became my own private detective, searching for what deadly disease I seemed to be infected with, feeling as useless and powerless as the act of abuse itself. If I could not face my abuser and figure out what truly happened, then I was going to prove to myself how unlovable I really was. This was easy evidence to find, as I seemed to muster up trouble at every turn I made, like a magnet to disappointment.

ભ

The summer before my sophomore year at Highland, my interest in dating flared up like it does with most teenagers. It was my brothers who schooled me on dating and the "love languages." The

Warner home was always abuzz with my brothers and their friends, playing "Pong" on the computer or watching *Dukes of Hazard*. Our parents surprised us one Christmas with a wonderful game room; so many games of pool, Ping-Pong, and foosball were exchanged as I observed how to connect through athletic competition. I learned how to easily communicate with young men, both verbally and through body language. I knew a slug on the arm or a nonchalant shrug of the shoulders meant, *I'm too cool to say it, but I think you're nice.* Interactions with the opposite gender became so automatic that I think I often unwittingly sent the wrong signals. Whenever a young man assumed we were more than friends when we hadn't done more than talk, I was taken aback (though flattered) and baffled how things went from A to C so quickly. My brothers later enlightened me on this truth: most guys don't do girl "friends," but usually have some ulterior motives, possibly because of their hormones. This theory was put to the test, and I began to view most men like the man who took away my innocence, as if they were never interested in the "real me," only what they could get from me. To protect my ego, I got into the habit of hurting them before they could hurt me.

About this same time at age 13, I had been put on a prescription of Prozac to temper my depression, but all it seemed to do was make me feel numb, estranging me from people around me like my church group. I knew the LDS church was true, but I thought everyone looked down on me because I liked boys and paid little attention to what the other girls in my Young Women's class were interested in, such as dancing and sewing. I was experiencing a temporary spiritual amnesia, seeking for identity past the residue of abuse.

My ward's (which is an individual congregation within the Church) youth program once had a goal to read the Book of Mormon (a companion to the Bible and another testament of Jesus Christ) together by a certain date. Feeling more resistant to conformity than usual, I refused to read it by the parameters they set, and ended up standing awkwardly off to the side in the celebratory photo for achieving the goal. I tended to avoid as many church activities as I could, which only served to draw the concern of my bishop (our congregation's ecclesiastical leader).

Bishop Calvin was much beloved in the ward and connected seamlessly to the youth, yet I was always uneasy around him. The vision I had for anyone with what I felt were "pushy" boundaries was that they were forcing me against my will, which wasn't always true. I just needed my space.

One afternoon my mom found me in the dining room and held the phone up to me, saying, "Bishop Calvin would like to talk to you." I told her to talk to him for me, as I would rather have my parents hear the poor behavior I was up to rather than let him ask me awkward questions. He had done this to me in our previous interviews.

I remember being called over to his home for a personal interview to see how I was doing, generally and with the standards of our gospel. He saw right through all my lies, but I didn't care. It had nothing to do with my loyalty to God, whom I truly loved and believed in. I was acting out and drawn to danger because it is where I felt most comfortable. I just wanted to run as far away as I could. I felt the Bishop was only seeing my outward rebellion, not the war inside of me. If I couldn't even understand what was happening in my soul, why would he be able to? Yes, he was inspired by God, but he was mortal, and the topic of abuse was not commonly discussed like it is now. It was overlooked more often than not at the time. I believe now that I was supposed to tread this path, so it was meant to be that my abuse was not addressed until much later in life. Like most of us though, Bishop Calvin did his best with what he knew at the time. I was simply spitting old venom on a new victim of my own, not realizing at the time that my harbored, angry feelings were truly for the man who started it all back in his exam room.

The abuse seemed to trump any attempts by my family, Young Women's leaders, or Bishop Calvin to teach me about my worth. I could see the worth in others, but it felt unreachable in someone like me who was so blemished. I was mad at the world, as if someone had said to me, "You're not going to Heaven anyway." The *Dark One*, or the adversary to God's plan, had iced my heart with this falsehood and lies. Misery loves company, and although I may not have meant to let him in at the time, it was the nature of my beastly side to open the door.

Although the truth of my pain would be within reach, the heaviness and poison of the past deadened any beauty trying to bud in my life, like a tulip sprouting in the spring only to be crushed in a late winter storm.

ଓ

Tension between my mom and me hardened like an old cake left on a shelf when I became a sophomore in high school. It was another power struggle, which felt as horrible as the abuse itself. I loved her, but the feeling of being boarded off to the island of misfits—with medication and silence—overshadowed any healthy connection we might have had. Car rides with Mom were pretty much dead silent, as if I was protesting: *you didn't hear me as a child, so now your words fall on deaf ears.*

Mom was bound and determined to try to salvage us, but the more she tried to put the pieces together, the faster they seemed to crumble. I was restless and fighting against a power I couldn't physically touch, and since she was there—tangible—I lashed out in raw, unrestrained rage. I knew that even if I focused all my blame on her, she would still love me regardless.

After packing my bags and hauling the two of us up to our family cabin at Mt. Air for a night or two of mother-daughter bonding, she informed me that we were not heading home just yet. She fixed our car due northeast towards Cheyenne. I threw a fit. It was one thing to suffer through two days without my friends, but now I was being kidnapped! I pouted out the passenger side window, as if my petrified heart could somehow turn the car around. Undeterred, Mom charged through the Rockies to Wyoming. My acting out was more than a typical spoiled brat, but we just didn't know it yet.

Surprisingly, while we were in Jackson a part of me let go. We stayed in these adorable cabins, and my icy heart slowly started to melt as we wandered up and down Main Street, browsing the shops. It was like we'd been launched back in time to quick-draw with the cowboys. We strolled down a wooden boardwalk, majestic, snowcapped mountains painted in the background. Mom bought me a beautiful, soft saddle leather jacket with a fur-trimmed hood. Just being a tourist for a time—nothing more or less—allowed my confused and defensive resentment to simmer down. But as soon as we left the quaintness of Main, Mom made a corrective comment about my grammar or my gum chewing, and my irritation froze over.

One special night we attended a true Western showdown at the Wort Hotel. Sounding too much like "wart," I thought it disgusting that someone would name a place after those awful blemishes I sometimes got on my knuckles and elbows. Whenever tensions arose—and to throw down the authoritarian card with my mom—I would call her "Nedra," and in return she would call me "Wart," knowing how much I hated the word. I quickly learned how disrespectful it was to refer to her this way, but underneath the warmth of my newly bought findings lay a revolving cycle of disconnect between us, which couldn't be solved in a weekend. Still, mom gets an A for effort, as she attempted to resolve things in her way of expressing love.

At home as the year progressed, conflict grew like morning glory on a rose bush, smothering any nutrients gained from the sun and rain. Mom wasn't singled out. I wanted *both* of my parents to acknowledge what had happened to me in that doctor's office—as to finally satisfy the dragon fuming at the brink of its cave and set me free—but I could sense they were too ashamed to talk about it. One afternoon, after months of dormancy, my emotional volcano erupted. Attempting to extinguish the raging fire in my heart, I lay burrowed under blankets in my room, crying and telling myself why I couldn't go to the Friday night football game. My parents came upstairs to check on me. I screamed at them, accusing them if they had any feelings at all about the abuse. Mom was perplexed and frightened. Dad exclaimed that if he could have hurt the doctor he probably would have; though I knew deep down, regardless of his loyalty to me, he couldn't hurt a fly. It did appease me for a moment, though. I stood puzzling over why mom seemed tongue-tied. It seemed like Dr. Strover's wife's feelings were more important than my own—because she had been a school friend—and so my voice was cut off from ever being heard at the risk of hurting her. My judgments to her would later be so completely countered to what was truly boiling up in that tender heart of hers. Some people simply don't know how to illustrate what they're feeling the way we need at the time.

It was one thing to feel alone as a child, but as a teen the doctor's office was embedded in the walls of my own home as an unspeakable secret. I wanted to feel validated, laying everything out on the table that had happened to me as a child. I felt that by keeping the truth a taboo subject—by asking me to take my medication when I acted out—my parents were denying that it had ever been real. There *was* pain in their hearts, mortar building up the walls of my own heart, but they couldn't convey that pain to the extent I grieved for. I would need to drain my own well of the poison, not theirs.

All this friction grated on me and I pushed blame on nearly everyone around me. I was blind to it at the time, but later I would realize how many prayers my family and friends sent to Heavenly Father on my behalf. A link of resentment anchored my heart to the depths of despair for a season. Gratefully, though, God saw my bitterness and gave me an avenue to filter the rage: sports.

Left: In junior high
Bottom Left: a
chalk drawing
Mom had painted
of me in New
Orleans, age 15
Bottom Right:
Mom and I

Link 4:

Coping From Abuse

"But they that wait upon the Lord shall renew their strength;
they shall mount up with wings as eagles; they shall run…"
~Isaiah 40:31

If you were a Warner at the age of three, then you were introduced to a racket and a tennis ball. Family reunions were held at the best courts, tournaments were a fifth food group, and table talk at dinner time served up more than just food—but dishes like who had won the "match of the day." We lived for the challenge of the solo game: a shrewd test of defense, offense, and endurance. Tennis taught us all of these, but above all, it taught us sportsmanship. If a Warner played with a discourteous attitude, the game would end quickly. Once, in a game of mixed doubles, my competitive brother Ned swung his racket with a little too much angst. Having none of that (and having warned Ned *twice* to switch up his attitude), Mom defaulted and walked off the court. The game was over. At that moment, a principle was embedded in my soul, more important than any win: tennis is about growth. Mom was one classy lady on and off the court, teaching us what truly made us winners in the game of life.

The green-lined, netted cement court was my greatest classroom. And my parents and siblings were my venerated teachers. I continually watched how they handled themselves in the thick of adversity. Whether it was an overly intense coach spouting intimidating mind-games from the sidelines, a biased linesman, or a seemingly unconquerable opponent, my family was taught how to play a fair game. For the Warner's, tennis was a time to bond together. It was an expression of our unspoken devotion for each other.

My father loved the game almost as much as he loved the gospel of Jesus Christ. He could weave inspiring spiritual principles into almost any match or practice. He taught me how to deal with conflict on and off the court, how to look past a poor referee call, and most importantly how to win friendship over a match. Hours of hot, sunny days were spent at the courts at Liberty Park playing "No-Champs" matches to prepare my siblings and me for our next tournament. In the wintertime, Dad would get us up (though he always said that *we* had to wake *him* up) early in the morning so we could practice at the Salt Lake City Tennis Club a mile away. I still remember Ned quietly opening my bedroom door and whispering, "Hey, Sis, if you want to go we're leaving in 15 minutes." As tired as I was, I knew I would be missing out on precious bonding time if I didn't go, so I rallied myself together and threw back the warm covers.

The arctic air shot ice through my lungs as I breathed and froze my scrawny legs as we hustled up the long walkway, but as soon as I stepped onto that indoor court, my whole body fired up. Number six was *our* court. The lights flicked on as we parted the heavy, forest green curtains as if announcing the Warner's were here to learn another invaluable life lesson.

My father knew how to have fun while influencing us for good. He taught us to love our opponent more than a win. He could correct our technique while simultaneously complimenting us. To this day, Ned continues Dad's legacy of teaching life's hardest lessons to his five children with a tennis ball and a racket. What a stud!

Learning side-by-side with Ned was life changing. I wanted to be like him. He was a powerful hitter yet had matchless finesse as he did a top spin off his forehead. His senior year at Highland High School,

Ned won state in doubles with our cousin Stayner Warner. Admiring his skill, strength, and determination, I often fantasized about being as great a player as my brothers—not just because of their trophies, but because of the character I could see building within the courts of their hearts.

Because of my petite form growing up, I had to learn how to strategize in order to win. With the scorching summer sun pouring down on us, my oldest brother Dave, an avid player himself, took my twelve-year-old self aside in the middle of a split set to give me some advice. "Peggy," he said, "you got this. All you need to do is keep lobbing back to your opponent. Wear her down, allow her to get her head in the game, and watch the magic happen. You don't have to wear yourself out by trying to slam her powerful shots—just be consistent in returning them, and stay mentally strong. She'll wonder what she doesn't know about your tenacity." This revelatory advice stuck with me not only through my successful tennis years, but throughout my entire life. Dave had wise foresight; I love him for this.

Throughout my teen years I used tennis, among other sports, as a coping mechanism. My days started out with those early morning tennis rallies and ended with a run lasting as long as my body would hold up. A few neighborhood friends would appease me by tagging along for a couple of miles. I was slow, but I could last like a tortoise in a race. I felt if I kept running long enough, I could outrun all my worries—like why that boy didn't like me, why I was failing that class, or why I would be so eager to leap from school to school like a frog in the years to come.

In the beginning I was ecstatic to attend Highland High School, the alma mater of all my siblings. Ned had graduated the year prior to my arrival, having won the "Nick Caputo Award" which applauded his participation in three different sports all four years of high school while maintaining a high GPA. I was immensely proud of my siblings, and yearned for their admiration. If I couldn't find acceptance from within, I sought it from without. Paradoxically, I wanted it most from the source of my pain: young men. Whether it came in the form of a healthy brotherly connection, or from the boys who asked me out, I was seeking what had been lost in that doctor's office: respect and genuine love.

One afternoon at the beginning of my ninth grade year, my brothers came downstairs after school to find me watching *Days of Our Lives* while eating a colossal bowl of Star Light mint chocolate chip ice cream with my Big Mac. It was the off-season for tennis, so I was content to relax after a grueling day of school. Appalled, they said, "Peggy. Get off that couch, grab your shoes, and come running with us. You're going to morph into a mushy blob if you don't change your habits." I was by no means pudgy, but this little bug my brothers had put in my ear built a nest, and my thoughts turned obsessive. I joined the track team and then later the cross-country team. I was achingly slow, but I heeded my brother Gill's advice: "Never slow down to a walk. If you do, it'll be harder to get going again." Even though these words would fuel an obsession, they would eventually be motivators as I faced down my darkest hours, wanting nothing more than to quit. Truly, these words foreshadowed more than a footrace.

Gill and Ned were training for their first triathlon and would let me tag along to swim or bike with them. When track season ended, my need for the endorphin rush continued. I signed up for any sort of athletic training, be it a weights class or aerobics, and even lifted with my brothers and their friends in a basement-turned-weight room. During spring break my sophomore year I went to a "fitness farm" (as I called it) at the base of Snow Canyon in St. George, Utah. I fibbed to the staff that I was training for a triathlon (yet I could hardly swim the length of the pool), because my 105 pounds wasn't quite the standard of their typical guests. While my friends lounged around a pool in

Green Valley, I was sweating through four workouts, and then biking some eight miles over desolate terrain before joining them.

I was fixated on making the reflection in the gym mirror perfect, curve-less, as if I could sweat away any signs of being a girl, even if I did not realize it at the time. My friends were worried about me; they called hotlines and even confronted me for an intervention. Looking back now, I can honestly say I had an excessive exercise disorder, as well as an eating disorder that drove me to work out immediately after I ate anything, no matter what other obligations I had. I found eating bothersome, and ate only to refuel. I shunned foods that would add fat to my hips, and learned how to replace greasy piecrust with Grape Nuts cereal. If I couldn't control the nightmare in my mind, at least I could control my physical body even if I couldn't recognize it.

I returned home with my newfound recipes and an intoxicating drive to work out every spare moment. I replaced my human relationships, which were risky and painful, with exercise, a relationship with a solid return. It didn't matter what kind of workout it was, so long as I could work up a good sweat it felt like nothing or no one could harm me in these moments. The tread of my fitness habits, no matter how extraneous or extreme, proved to me one thing: I was running from more than weight gain, and sooner or later the track would end. One day I would need to find the courage to strike Goliath down instead of trying to run from him and all my insecurities.

Around Christmastime my sophomore year, Goliath returned as the pervasive feeling of wanting out. I was taking my anti-depressants on and off, but they would only tame the beast within for so long. Trials were piling up on my family's doorstep, and I was feeling crowded out of home by my seeming inability to live up to my siblings' successes.

I picked up my feet to run again, looking in the direction of my trusted childhood friend Alecia Thompson and her family, who had since moved from our neighborhood. My mother had taught me the metaphor of the golden windows, where we sometimes gaze across a valley and see others' windows shimmering with the effulgent sunset, lit up like gold. We think their lives must be perfect, unhampered by trials or trouble of any kind. I saw the Thompsons through a golden window.

I transferred schools to Skyline High and asked Alecia if I could live with her family for the remainder of my sophomore year. Even though it broke her heart, Mom let me go stretch out my wings—as any good mother would do when her child inched to the edge of the nest. Each morning she'd call to tell me she loved me and to have a great day at school, knowing in her heart I'd one day remember the rest of the metaphor: When you are on the other side of the valley looking back, you will see that the sun still radiates, casting light on your own sparkling windows. My attempt to link my soul to a new pace of life would prove to reflect more than the fable taught. It would give insight to the problem that didn't lie within my own home, but within the walls of my heart.

My family, playing tennis

Link 5:

Prodigal Daughter

"And the [daughter] said unto him, Father, I have sinned against heaven, and in thy sight, and am no more worthy to be called thy [daughter]. But the father said to his servants...this my [daughter] was dead, and is alive again; [she] was lost, and is found." ~Luke 5:20-24

I loved the Thompson family. They welcomed me in as one of their own daughters, fed me, gave me a bed, and even assigned me weekly chores. Alecia's parents resembled the couple in the drama *Hart to Hart*, which I'd faithfully watch every Friday night right after *Dallas*, while tending for a family in the neighborhood. Kathy, Alecia's mom, was a keen, beautiful, and intelligent woman. She quickly caught onto my exercise fetish and scary eating habits, and in her motherly way restricted me to only one workout per day. One month passed, and then two, and pretty soon the truth that I'd run so far from caught up to me. As much as I loved the Thompsons, I still felt restless.

This revelation hit me at lunch one day. While I was eating one of Kathy's irresistible turkey sandwiches, I had this feeling that I was headed into No Man's Land. To tennis players, No Man's Land is the space between the service line and the base line; if you're standing there too long you might get caught in the direct bounce of the ball and tangle up your feet, which are your foundation, and throw off your return placement. I realized I shouldn't be trying to live someone else's life. The Thompsons looked like they had it all together, and I thought living with them would pacify the battle inside me, but relocating hadn't solved anything. My feelings had followed me like a bad rash.

I think Kathy knew this intuitively before I ever did. Life as a Thompson was as normal as life as a Warner—homework and chores and all—and I was subtly nudged back into my own nest (which I now sincerely thank the Thompsons for). So there I was, back to where I started, free to run the pavements for as long as I liked, but still facing a power struggle with my parents.

Strangely, I now desired the feeling I had had at Carden, with the small classrooms and focused attention from the faculty I had so passionately resisted in my younger years. After seeking out a private school called Rowland Hall-St. Marks, I talked to my parents and suggested that transferring there might help me get my act together, as I was a bit free-spirited at Skyline. With the movie *Dead Poets Society* as my ideal, I hoped for that kind of richness in my last two years of high school. In time, links in my chain of trials would come into clear view, strengthening me as I recognized that I might be more connected to God than I had thought.

Rowland Hall was an Episcopalian school. Being a member of the Church of Jesus Christ of Latter-day Saints, I was immediately singled out. I didn't mind. As a result of constantly resisting control, I loved going against the grain. When before I had been impartial, I found myself sticking up for the LDS church whenever students from out of state, not used to Utah's culture, would complain about the closed stores on Sundays or poke fun at our doctrines. Instead of isolating myself in the majorities as I had done at Highland and Skyline, I openly shared my feelings with my questioning classmates. I was now speaking out for the team I had resisted up till this point.

One day as I was pulling textbooks from my locker, a fellow senior named Mia came up to me and asked if I was truly considering serving a mission for my church. I had before casually mentioned to a few friends that I'd jump on the chance. In disgust, she went on to say, "You mean you'd really take 18 months out of your life, not getting paid but actually *paying your own way* to teach others about your faith? Sounds insane..." I knew she was calling me out on my declaration, and in that moment a question I'd never really asked myself before rocked my nerves: *What* do *I truly believe?*

After a long, earnest pause, I replied, "I'm not sure what the future will bring, but I want to be worthy if I'm ever prompted to serve."

Even though I was a fair weather friend in attending seminary (an LDS class taught off campus as an elective) at Highland and Skyline, I was drawn to attend at East High School, which was about six blocks east of Rowland (as Rowland didn't offer it). I could drive there and get back in time for ceramics class if I was careful not to fly too fast down 8th South—getting a ticket on those bumpy Wasatch hills we teenagers loved to try to catch air on.

There was an instant connection between our teacher, Sister Taylor, and me. She was a darling pregnant lady who seemed to have this whole "life" thing down. She knew the scriptures inside and out, and was effective in relating them to her students, inspiring us to become better sons and daughters of God. I was realizing how childish and lonely my days of rebelliousness had been, and I found myself longing to be more like Sister Taylor. I wanted to become a mother like she was. I wanted the cleanliness she seemed to exude from her soul. She was teaching us through example the principles of the gospel of Christ, which were all of the attributes my mom emulated, yet because of the tension between us I failed to connect to them.

My soul was awakening as if this was the first time I was hearing all these incredible ideas about a Savior who died for *me*, so that I might start anew and have eternal life. What had been fed to me every Sunday over the past 17 years of my life now seemed new and magnificent, simply because it was coming from Sister Taylor. She had a gift of reaching her hand out to the frightened, caged animal inside me and cajoling it into meekness. The saying, *you water a bush for five years and on the sixth year it grows fully*, was parallel to the small, mustard seed of a testimony tenderly being cultivated in my heart.

With the control of authority clipped out of my life, my connection to God was sprouting. Even though my parents, a well-intentioned Bishop, and countless selfless Young Women's leaders had tried to teach me the same concepts just as gracefully, it took someone outside my range of pain deflection to ignite a dormant spark of hope, buried under encrusted layers of protection.

I must have had a glowing countenance about me (other than sweaty hormones) when I'd enter the ceramics room the next period, because soon a few of my friends were asking questions about what I had learned that day in Seminary. My friend Matt, who was an expert in the art of snide remarks, would call it "Semitary." Knowing how snarky he was, I would kid back to help him keep up his image of "cool," but secretly I knew he was genuinely interested. As I began trusting him with my heart and shared the latest lessons with him, my testimony of the gospel was steadily strengthening.

Being a staff member on the school newspaper gave me an opportunity to share my beliefs with the whole student body, though at first I resisted joining (needing an elective credit won out in the end). As I began writing for the school, something unlocked in me. I found myself writing poetry, and all my stunted, moody feelings poured out onto paper as newfound release. Dark and depressing thoughts flooded endless sheets of paper as if I had opened a Pandora's Box of emotions. Writing—and art, as I had a talent for painting soft landscapes in layered pastels—helped me sift through my conflicted heart. With each blank sheet and clean canvas, I was able to craft with my hands what my tongue could not articulate.

When I was asked to write a piece for the newspaper on how a Mormon (a nickname for our faith) could coincide at an Episcopalian school, I felt I was summoned by the Savior to fight for His cause. I still had a *long* way to go in becoming like the girls in my Young Women's group, but the Lord knew me and He knew how I would respond to the challenge of being a minority. It was as if the Lord was using reverse psychology on me. For someone who had been stripped of free will, feeling in control of the moment is a lifeline, even if that control is an illusion. The Lord was providing me, on my terms, an opportunity to be in control of my reactions, beliefs, and responses to others questioning my faith.

After my article had been printed, another classmate named Cameron, whom I had semi-dated and ended on poor terms with, called me out on my typed testament, saying I had sounded pompous. He knew, almost as well as I did, the "rules" of my religion, and he knew I had not been as faithful in keeping them as I should have.

Struck, I admitted, "You're right. I have made many mistakes and probably will continue to as I learn more about myself. But I believe in the Atonement of Christ. If I repent with a humble heart while stopping the unwanted behavior, I can be forgiven."

The hallway was so quiet you could have heard a mouse sneeze. Those words, which had so unashamedly come out of my mouth, penetrated my heart, and I felt the Spirit touching Cameron's heart as well. I believe this moment foreshadowed the work the Lord had in store for me to come. I didn't want to take a newspaper class or even be a school jumper, but the Lord knows what's best for us and He sees in us the potential of who we are meant to become in this earthly life.

This crucial moment of owning my mistakes and finding grace in my Savior's sacrifice was a turning point, guiding me to find my earthly purpose. Truth and righteousness burned within me as more and more questions were directed my way, and as I defended His message I began to find links to possible ways of healing, not only in print but also in voice.

Friends from high school

Link 6:

Potential for Success

*"A good coach will make [her] players see
what they can be rather than what they are."*
~Ara Parasheghian

Before I even started at Rowland Hall I was asked to join the tennis team. This seemed a bit rash, I thought, as I had only been an alternate on Highland High's team my freshman and sophomore years. I knew the winds had changed in my favor when I was given the spot of 2nd doubles in a phone call with the coach. This showed just how desperate he must have been for players, as I was not a grand-slam hitter. That season my partner and I did pretty fair, but a desire to reach higher took root. Being a senior meant I had one more year of adolescence before adulthood took over. More than that, it meant I only had one more year to prove myself. With my brother Ned already a state tennis champion, I wished to prove I was just as capable of becoming someone strong enough to win it all.

A new year meant a new coach, and unlike Rowland's coach for junior year—a spirited, foreign gentleman with distressing intensity— I immediately loved her. Coach Lisa Halversen knew how to inspire her players and stretch us to our limits. She instilled in us the dream of exceeding last year's potential and planted the seed of limitless possibilities in our hearts. She did more than coach us. She believed in us. She believed in *me*.

One afternoon, our third team player for the singles player-on-player match didn't show. I was still on the roster to play doubles, though my heart had been aching to play singles for quite some time now. In a bold move, I asked Coach Halversen if I could fill in for the absentee player. I looked into her face, hoping, and could tell she was torn. I wasn't the most skilled player she'd seen at tryouts, but I had made the team nonetheless. Maybe it was my unyielding, imaginary confidence brimming off my shoulders, or the dread of having to forfeit the match if she couldn't find a substitute. Either way, Coach Halversen gave me a chance.

I was in no way an ace server. But I had the gift of tenacity and endurance taught to me by my brothers and father. Steady as a mountain, I knew how to scurry after the ball and return shots until my opponent started to wear down. Fortunately, I was able to pull that match off, proving worthy of a permanent spot in singles. Coach Halversen's belief in me wasn't wasted. I won that singles match and the majority of the matches afterwards, which led me to represent my team at the State Championships. Links of potential greatness were within reach, even if this was a mortal way of finding self-worth.

"Stay steady," Ned reminded me before I stepped onto the court. I bounced on my toes, teeming with the adrenaline pumping through me. This would be the last match in my tennis career, as I wasn't planning on playing in college. If I was going to prove I had my brother's capacity for being a champion in the sport, it would have to be now.

The tension was hot. I felt all my rallies and hard work had built up to this very moment. But I knew that if I thought too much about it I'd lose focus, so I kept my head in the game and did what I'd done all season: consistently returning the ball. We were on the last spot of four courts, surrounded by a 12-foot high chain link fence. The green mesh curtain above our heads swayed as the breeze helped lob our volleys over the net. I had the advantage of playing my opponent previous times in the season, so I was aware of how to push and back off according to her temperament.

With every hit and return I could feel her getting more intense. She wanted to win this as much as I did. Each time we switched sides after a set, I watched her rub the head of her lucky monkey which hung by its Velcro arms on the side of the net. She glanced over at her coach, as if pleading for him to give her some secret weapon to help her pull out on top in the final set. Up to this point, our rallies had pushed the score back and forth like a tooth ready to be pulled. Just when I thought I was closing in, she'd whip out a new resolve and bring the score back to 30-all.

Coach Halversen (who was now more of a friend than a mentor), Ned, and my parents were within reach, cheering me on. Dad looked like he did at most athletic events—pacing back and forth on the sidelines—while mom gave me her smile of "You've got this Peggy! Go for it!" Dad opened up his suit coat, and pinned inside was his coined phrase: "You Gotta Believe!" Ned leaned on the fence, my focus on the tight rope so I wouldn't look down as the last set was played. He would study my opponent's moves and then give me advice on strategy. He nodded to me and held up a fist. *Calm and steady.* I felt his confidence in me. I had come out on top in three other matches against this same opponent this year, and I was proving to myself that I had the skill to win, or at least the desire within. The secret was to focus on what I could control—my responses—and not allow my eagerness to jump ahead, distracting me from being fully present.

My opponent served first, allowing her anxiety to drive the ball right into the net. She shook it off, but I could tell she was upset. Again and again she let her frustration fuel her shots. It was almost as if she was handing me the game with her unbridled passion and fear of letting her coach down. She was getting tired; with a final swing of my racket I forced the ball over the net and past her reach, claiming the final points of the match.

My family pulled me into a Warner victory hug, shouting, "You won!"

"I got lucky," was my reply, though I was beaming. *I won!* I had done it. I was building a pool of proof that I was more than a washed-up rebellious teen and had something of worth to give back to the school and world that seemed to misunderstand me. I felt like I was contributing for once, instead of being the outcast with a cankered soul.

I looked across the court at my opponent, burying her face in her mother's shoulder, the rest of her family gathered around her in consolation.

"She's a junior. She'll get another chance next year," Ned assured me. Sympathy was visible on my face, my excitement at taking state considerably lessened. I realized all the tennis titles I had earned were not as important as proving my sportsmanship. If I left an opponent less than a friend, then I had not won a triumph, simply gained a hunk of metal that would tarnish on the shelf in a few years.

I found her later, crying into her knees on a narrow strip of grass facing the courts. Sitting down next to her, I wrapped one arm around her shaking shoulders and told her what an incredible player she was to have made it all the way to state. I thanked her for the challenging season and wished her luck on her senior year.

"Thank you," she said, smiling.

No longer opponents, we left the courts as friends.

My quest to find potential had been born out of perseverance and a belief in myself that if I stuck something out long enough—with a glimpse of hope—there would be numerous opportunities. Even if the trophy would tarnish over time, my inner voice would strengthen.

Years later, I would see how crucial this life lesson would be when I faced life's hardest opponent of all: the will to live.

Left: Coach Lisa Halverson, the one who believed in me
Bottom: Tennis, senior year at Rowland Hall

Link 7:

Sisterhood Love

"Charity suffereth long, and is kind; charity envieth not; charity vaunteth not itself, is not puffed up."
~1 Corinthians 13:4

Graduating from Rowland Hall felt like a dreamy wedding ceremony. I wore a white dress and followed my classmates down a red carpet, carrying a dozen long-stemmed roses. I wasn't a frilly-dress girl back then, but I longed to feel special. And that day I definitely did, if only for a brief moment.

As I strolled down the aisle of the ornate Episcopalian church, I glanced at the many faces of proud parents and congratulatory relatives, amazed that they were there for *me* as much as the other 44 graduates. I most likely wouldn't see my classmates ever again, yet I was grateful for the lessons I had learned with them as we began discovering ourselves one layer at a time. As we reflected on our mistakes and the inescapable awkwardness of high school, we recognized how much we had bonded despite our unique backgrounds. We were each excited to watch each other soar out of the nest and see what our wings could do.

I was a tad embarrassed that most of the graduates were moving on to Ivy League colleges, which is what our prep school had prepared us to do, while I would be staying close to home. I had this vision of attending Purdue University with its colorful hills and *Dead Poets*

Society feel. I would later find out that attending the University of Utah was more than just a gut feeling, but that God had a bigger university waiting for me called "Life."

◌

My mom and both my sisters had been involved in Greek sororities during their college days, and they were excited for me to join one, too. But I had no desire to go there. *A sorority?* I thought. *That is so beneath me.* Due to past experiences, girls my age weren't exactly in my good graces, nor I in theirs. And the thought of my being surrounded by anyone who might remind me of the "mean girls" in school just didn't appeal. Secretly, though, I was really just scared of not fitting in. Mom, who had been the first president of the LDS sorority Lambda Delta—and loved it with all her heart, serving in the organization for 25 years—insisted I rush.

Being around immensely spiritual people always made me feel a bit lost, like they could see through my skin to all the mistakes I had made and kept buried in my bones. I was the lost lamb in Jesus's parable, because I felt I wasn't quite on their spiritual level yet.

I watched every skit put on by the sororities during Rush Week. The last one, presented on the LDS institute campus by a group called Gamma Xi (which was also a church sorority), drew me in. They seemed to have a creative combination for classy and cool as they performed. I looked around at the other hopeful young women in the audience, and some of them looked back at me with nervous eyes as if saying, *Will we find a place to fit in?* As the chapter members bowed and we applauded, I made up my mind that this was the group I'd attempt to join.

"But I'll only turn in my letter of intent for *this* group," I told my mom. Boy, I was conceited, to say the least.

When the time came to find out who had been accepted into Gamma Xi, I had to admit to myself that there were butterflies in my stomach. All sorority applicants packed into lines leading up to a table where Gamma Xi sisters searched for our names on the master list of inductees. There was a girl in the line next to me, and we reached the table at the same time. I heard her give her name, Julie Debry, and heard the staff member reply, "I'm sorry, Gamma Xi is full. You will have to go with your next choice."

As Julie's countenance fell, my heart welled with compassion and my voice spilled out. "If Julie doesn't get in, then I won't either," I said, though I was just told I was accepted. In that short moment of empathy I had for her, I felt a deep connection between us, like we were kindred spirits. Somehow I knew we were going to be instant friends with the kind of relationship that never wanes or tires. I knew immediately that if Julie wasn't going to be there, then I wasn't meant to join. Behind me, a girl seconded my declaration, and another behind her. We weren't going to join Gamma Xi without Julie.

Julie was warm and sincere with a contagious laugh, and one of the best sisters Gamma Xi ever had. We seized freshman year with fearlessness and vigor, double dating and attending Gamma Xi's activities, such as the Barn Dance. She was my twin, helping me look inside to find my true self. She later shared this truth with me, giving me a plaque that read: "We all let people into our lives, but you will find that really good friends let you into your own."

All the sisters of Gamma Xi, including my longtime friend Ashley Brooks, and a new friend named Amy Iverson, helped illuminate my individual worth. I felt my testimony grow as the walls of my barricaded heart were diminishing. Sharing my tender feelings with these girls at our weekly meetings opened up a chamber in my heart I didn't know was there. I was starting to trust again. Trust other girls. Trust our unforgettable leader, Joyce Buehner, who led our groups with such confidence and peace that I knew I was *home*. I was in awe of our president and her counselors. I wanted to be just as courageous in testifying the truths of the gospel as they were.

The following year I became a Pledge Trainer, inviting our staff to the family cabin where we planned the skits for next year's Rush Week. I was blessed to know each of those girls individually, and as I learned of their struggles and heartaches, my heart ached with them. I discovered how my impressions of spiritual women were clouded by the way I was judging myself. I realized that those "mean girls" in school might have been hurting just like I was. Even though the Goliaths in our lives came in different forms, we were the *same* in that we had to face them, one stone at a time.

I was changing! My own links were connecting to others' who had also risked opening up their protected hearts so that they, like me, might become stronger.

Me with my niece Ruby (Nancy's daughter who
lived with us for three years of her life and
became like a sister to me)

Senior year, graduation day

Top: Gamma Xi LDS sorority (our theme for rush was "Come Fly with Gamma Xi!)
Left: Me with Julie Labrum, 1994, Gamma Xi Halloween Dance

Trust in Unanswered Prayers

"Whosoever shall put their trust in God shall be
supported in their trials, and their troubles, and their
afflictions, and shall be lifted up at the last day."

~Alma 36:3

I love the song "Unanswered Prayers" by George Straight because of its irony. Sometimes what we think is the right course might actually lead us down a lonely road. In His omniscience, the Lord can see around each bend and turn, knowing what obstacles we'll face as individuals or as families. He knows exactly what we'll need in those dire straits. In my nineteenth year, this was a lesson taught to my heart.

Along the road to discovering new healthy connections with my gender, I continued to be the girl attracted to the heartbreaker. I did not see back then how the abuse reinforced this thread of attracting the wrong kind of attention. I was blessed to have been asked out by really great guys in high school and college, yet my beacon seemed to land me smack dab into attracting what my abuse was expressing. I did not feel worthy of being treated like a princess, so any young man who was good to me I felt must be off in some way. The abuse had altered my girlish dreams of Happily Ever After and pulled me towards the outlaw instead of Prince Charming. If I could conquer the person least likely to see my worth, I thought I could somehow magically transform my belief system of worthlessness. However, it only collected more false evidence that I *was* worthless. The young men who were in as unhealthy a state as I was reacted with my lack of self-esteem, making our combination an explosive and volatile science experiment.

Feeling the day-by-day throb of heartbreak was something I was familiar with, especially when the ache involved dishonest boyfriends. But this pain was more raw and exquisite than I'd ever felt before.

His name was Derrick. My sorority sister lined us up for a date, if only to get closer to him herself (funny how confused girls work the system). Derrick was a dark haired, brown-eyed Chicagoan with a confidence reminding me of my brothers. He was 25, and Dad did not approve. Dad was leery of Derrick from the time I made introductions. Of course, this only made Derrick more mysterious and attractive. Though baffled why Dad didn't approve of us together, I clung to Derrick's arm in defiance, despite how much I adored my father.

When it came to Derrick, I feel as though I was seeking a quest to conquer something unattainable, like if I could tame or corral something so wrong for me, then all my dragons of the past would be defeated. Derrick was more than wrong for me, as together we seemed to ignite the unhealthy parts of each other. Apart, we were equally good in the sight of God, but together we were an equation of confusion that disconnected us from our true selves. We equaled the disjointed sum of two people completely lost in our quests of self-discovery, stuck in an explosive room of firecrackers.

After nine months of dating, we discussed marriage, picked out the rings, and planned a tentative wedding date. The only thing we hadn't done was pray about it, which should have been my clue that something was off. My young, naïve mind couldn't fathom any answer other than "yes."

Derrick proposed we take a weekend to fast and pray about it before finalizing anything. He went up to Ogden to be with a brother, who would help him hone his feelings. As for myself, I don't really think I knew how to "hone in" to anything other than what I felt was a sincere, occasional prayer here and there. I was so caught up in getting out on my own that I didn't truly *know* if Derrick was the right fit for eternity. He had been known for leaving a trail of hearts behind him, and I was flattered we had come this far. My intentions for driving this nail to alter may have been more for a victory of the ego than of the heart.

I had a habit of bending over backwards to please whoever I was with, even my friends. I wanted to make sure I was the kind of person no one would want to abandon. As such, I tended to carry the whole of the relationship on my back without realizing it. I understand now that I wasn't really in search of a good match; rather, I was trying to pacify my urgency to disprove how I wasn't worthy of being loved. We tend to date those whom we feel we deserve, and up to this point in my life I seemed magnetized to the hard-to-get young men, as if conquering the emotionally unavailable would be the ultimate proof of worth which I couldn't see clearly in the mirror. I thought that if I could make things work with Derrick—fighting all promptings from the Lord to find myself before I found the one to marry—my life would magically transform, leaving all pain behind.

That Sunday, there was a church fireside for all Young Single Adults. Derrick picked me up, but before we drove to the ward house he took me to a park above the zoo, perched in front of a gorgeous, August sunset. Giddy, I thought: *This is it!* He's going to propose!

"Peggy," he started, and I held my breath, "this doesn't feel right." I blinked at him, my chest crushed under the weight of a semi-truck. I stared out the passenger window, unable to comprehend what was happening. And when I took a double look at Derrick, the rejection hit with full force.

At the fireside, I barely heard a word out of the motivational speaker's mouth. The strident sound of my heart shattering to pieces drowned out everything else. Was I not good enough for him? Was it our age gap—which he had made reference to so many times? Every question my mind raised stung like nettle.

It wasn't until the phone rang at 5:30 the next morning when I considered the Lord may see a different path for me. Mom came into my room, phone in hand, saying Derrick was on the line. "He's going to reconsider," she said. "I know it." Sure enough, Derrick asked me to meet up with him, as he had had a change of heart. Pride frothed inside me. I was *not* going to be humiliated again. To prove this, I had already accepted a date offer from a fellow who had been nudging me for several weeks. I felt numb and hopeless, but I said yes anyway.

Derrick came over later that day to convince me his gauge might have been off. Even though I knew deep down he was right to put a halt to our progress, I felt a surge of anger and resentment similar to the antipathy I had had in the past for all men. "I don't know anymore," I told him, and then I said I had a date coming soon, so he needed to go.

For the next five months we played this game of Ping Pong, except now it was me pulling back on the reigns as we inched closer and closer again to a proposal. At every step, I sought the Lord, humbly now, in prayer. Each time I said "amen" it became harder and harder to imagine an eternity with Derrick. It all felt bleak, yet I didn't have the guts like he did at the beginning to just stick with our original thought of *this is not a good fit*. My fear of letting go prevented me from following promptings from the Holy Ghost (a comforter spirit sent by God) to cut ties before we made a major mistake. We were allowing ourselves to be led by our attractions for each other, not by God who knew what was really best for us, so the relationship continued according to our free will.

I even flew back to Chicago that Christmas to meet his family. One night his mother got me alone in the kitchen and confronted me about why I wouldn't marry her son. I was honest with her. "I feel I love your son," I said, "but I can't see an eternity together." If you've ever seen a mother bear protecting her cubs, that's what the tension felt like in the air, thick and fearsome enough to choke me as I—as casually as possible—gulped down some water. I didn't know how to express what Derrick and I both knew was not a healthy relationship. Yet we were used to each other's physical presence in our lives, and so the addiction was hard to break.

A little bird had been chirping in my ear since October to join the Brigham Young University Study Abroad group to Israel, and I was preparing to leave in January. I needed a time out to see things with new eyes. Derrick would be moving to Las Vegas, and I knew he'd be dating up a storm because he was a Casanova kind of guy, sleek and charming. My nerves hackled with jealousy, yet we both knew that letting go would bring more peace than remaining stagnant, ignoring the promptings that this was not right in the sight of the Lord. God had other plans for me. So I went to Israel, heartsick but trusting that Heavenly Father would make sense of my life one day.

༄

Israel was incredible. The rough desert terrain of the Holy Land sunk into my young bones like a soothing balm. BYU's Jerusalem Center was built on a breathtaking hillside with terraces embracing the rocky desert. At night, the white limestone glowed with celestial lights, earning the nickname "The City Upon a Hill" by the locals. Each room had a private balcony where you could bask in the hot, arid atmosphere, observing the Old City of Jerusalem from above. Just a few miles from our temporary home on the hillside lay Golgotha, where Christ was crucified, and the Garden Tomb, where He was laid to rest.

January of 1993 proved chilly as we ventured out to explore the Old City. Several camouflaged soldiers patrolled Herod's Gate as we entered, hefting machine guns on their shoulders. I innocently asked what the word *intifada* meant, having heard it spoken. My roommate's hand flew to my mouth and she rushed, "Shush, Peggy! If you say that word too loud, we'll have another Holy War on our hands!" I later learned it meant "war," and that Herod's Gate was one of the most contentious gates in the city where religious arguments could ignite at the mention of a single word, thus the need for double the guard.

At times, I felt I was facing a Holy War of my own, but despite the dangers outside the gates, Jerusalem flourished. People hustled through the dusty streets, checking wares methodically arranged and displayed by eager vendors. We were instructed to stay in groups of two or more.

With my fabulous roomies, Shauna Hall, Lynette Todd, and Laura Jacobson (whom I grew to love like family), I reverently strolled along the same pebbled streets Jesus might have 2,000 years ago. We searched for that perfect olive wood nativity set, or the local shekel earrings; you could buy three pairs for what we assumed was a pretty fair price. I feel I became an expert haggler. The trick was balance, not falling for the first or even third price offered by the shopkeeper. I would slowly shake my head, as if saying, "I'm moving on to the next vendor for a better offer." "Okay, okay!" the salesman conceded, lowering the price once again. I loved this tennis volley of bargaining more than the trinkets themselves, as it built a rapport between our two cultures.

The locals knew who we were, yet we were forbidden to preach the gospel of Jesus Christ as an arrangement with the government for being there. If we wanted to make a home in the midst of a Holy War, we needed to heed the warnings. Still, shopkeepers would call out to us—"Mormons!"—as we passed. One day I asked them how they knew us. "By the light in your eyes," they each said in turn. It was one of the sweetest compliments I had ever heard, and I knew it was true even if I hadn't always been the best example of a Christlike person. Day after day as my classmates and I immersed ourselves in the gospel of Christ and learned His doctrine, His light illuminated our countenances, even the dark corners of mine.

Midway through our experience I was asked to give the class a report on the Garden of Gethsemane (no pressure, right?). As I studied and prepared, my love for the Savior grew. I was treading the same paths He did in my own worn-out Israeli sandals, the same sand seeping between my toes. I couldn't deny the incredible witness of Gethsemane, barely an inkling of the bitter agony the Savior tasted as he bled from every pore, an atonement for my sins.

Early in the morning, we hiked over mounds of rocks into the Garden. Olive trees thousands of years old freckled the landscape, piquing the question if one of them was witness to the Savior's sacrifice for us. I had regrettably chosen to wear the traditional gypsum pants I'd purchased in the Old City. As the sun rose, the pants became see-through, baring my legs as silhouettes. Not only was I perspiring out of nervousness for my presentation, but on top of that I was terrified my classmates would laugh at the sheerness of my pants!

Suddenly, my concern for the pants shifted to the transparency of my soul. Attempting to convey the miracle that took place some 2,000 years prior felt like the ultimate hypocritical gesture. I felt so undeserving of the Savior's sacrifice. For me—who felt like the most blemished, weak, and least deserving of all the students in our group—to be presenting on the event which redeemed all mankind was an oxymoron. But was it really? As the words left my uncertain mouth, peace was whispered to my heart: Jesus Christ had bled those great droplets especially for persons with my past. I was the very kind

He atoned for, the ones whose sins were as scarlet, yet could be made as white as snow. Was it divine inspiration for me to have been asked to preach on what I had not yet taken advantage of in my own life? You bet. Just like any crumbling foundation, sometimes our walls must be demolished and a new, stronger foundation laid down. So, too, was my soul broken and rebuilt.

The Spirit felt tangible as we wandered through this serene sanctuary. I perched myself on a rock in the back of the Garden, looking out towards Golgotha and envisioning Christ's crucifixion. Right behind the spot was a bus station, separated by a mere wall of stone. I was shocked and irritated, wondering how people could build such a trite port of transportation next to this hallowed monument. Then one of my professors shared with me how, in biblical times, crucifixions took place where all people could see (and also mock and scorn), so for Golgotha to still be standing as the hub of where the locals congregate supports its importance, especially with Jesus' tomb so close by.

I found solace in Gethsemane and dreaded leaving it. I missed Derrick, but my heart ached because my prayers weren't being answered the way I hoped they would. All this confusion was fluttering in my mind about whether I should marry him or part ways for good. We had opportunities to talk periodically, and once I told him I was considering going on a mission when I turned 21.

"Wait," he said. "Please don't decide anything until you come home and we get a chance to see how things go between us."

"Okay," I answered, though in my heart I could feel this train wreck of a relationship was going to make its last stop. As layers of understanding peeled away, it became clear why it was necessary to put space between us. We needed to be apart in order to hearken to Heavenly Father's wisdom, instead of our hormones. We both needed to connect to a deep spiritual place before being capable of making such a powerful and altering decision such as marriage.

Before Israel, Derrick and I had landed ourselves in my new bishop's office way too many times for mistakes we had made in our conduct. However, the bishop was kind and drew me in with his "hands off" approach—which I appreciated. I never felt pressured or put down. I felt like things were on my terms, if only because my state of mind had changed from the times when I met with Bishop Calvin, making me more open and willing to give my will over to the Lord.

The truth that my relationship with Derrick was coming to an end—combined with the fact that I had temporarily stopped taking my anti-depressants because I hated how numb I felt on them—made me noticeably irritable in Israel.

"You don't like men very much do you," one of my classmates said to me as we bounced in a bus along the rocky back hills behind Bethlehem. Wes stood over 6'4" and spoke in a funny Canadian accent. He was always friendly, but like with a majority of the guys on the study abroad, I was prickly with him. I realized that even overseas my negative attitude had followed me, spotlighting the fact that it might not be the person across from me with the issue, but the person I saw in the mirror. I resisted anyone who got close to me to prevent getting hurt, reversing the role to be the abuser and not the victim.

Frustrated and feeling defeated by own confusion, I replied, "No, but it's not personal." Yet even when I felt landlocked and unable to determine which path led to joy and which to misery, Heavenly Father knew how to succor me. He gave me experiences in the Holy Land that answered my prayers in ways I had never expected. The links that held me captive in the past were breaking, providing a space for my heart to connect to the divine within me once again. Learning to trust God with my heart required planting a tiny yet powerful seed. My will was slowly becoming His.

Amy, Me, and
Julie, the day
before I left for
Israel

Israel Roomies:
Layette Todd, Me,
Laura Jacobson,
and Shauna Hall

Link 9:

Peace in the Holy Land

"These things I have spoken unto you, that in me ye might have peace. In the world ye shall have tribulation: but be of good cheer; I have overcome the world."

~John 16:33

One Sunday, my roommates and I were invited with a few other rooms of girls to attend a special dinner with a couple on the Jerusalem Center service missionary staff. The late Truman Madsen and his lovely, knowledgeable wife Ann hosted us in their quaint apartment, close to the Center's cafeteria. As we were introducing ourselves, we were asked to share with everyone why we felt we were led to Israel at this time in our lives. As I listened to the various answers flowing from my classmates, a revelatory thought came into my mind, blurting from my mouth out of turn.

"I'm here for my children," I proclaimed. Shocked with myself, I said it again with even more punch. "I'm here for my children! They need me to learn truth and wisdom, so that when they come, I can teach them." Peace rushed over me in that moment, as if the words I spoke were whispered in my ear by Heavenly Father, or even my potential children. He had a mission for me. He needed me to start letting go of the past and learn to trust Him, as well as myself.

Even though motherhood felt oceans away, never before had I been surer about my future. Love for my children began forming as if they were kindred souls waiting to reunite with me. It was a bond so secure that they were willing to put out warning signs when I was chasing the wrong dream, guiding me back to the path I was meant to walk.

Near the end of this enriching six-month experience, several of my classmates and I were blessed to have our parents visit. I felt like I had been away on a mission, if only to convert my own heart to the Savior's truths. Seeing Mom and Dad in their little hotel across the street from the Jerusalem Center was like my homecoming. Through their letters I learned how much they had to sacrifice in order for me to take part in this spiritual adventure, and when they travelled across the world to the Holy Land just to see me, I realized how important they really were to me and me to them.

We planned a special program for our visitors. Each student with parents visiting chose a favorite hymn from our Church's hymnbook, explained why it touched his or her heart and connected us, and then we all sang it together. I felt my choice was unique. That day, during a sacrament meeting that touched my heart, I looked out over the Old City as the hymn "Where Can I Turn for Peace?" began to play. My search was over. I knew immediately that would be the song I wanted to share with the parents. It wasn't until reviewing it, however, right before I went up to the pulpit, that I realized why it had touched me on so many levels.

"The arrangement and words are profound in describing what the Holy Land means to me," I spoke to the congregation, "but more importantly, this song is very dear to my heart because as I looked down to highlight the song title in my hymnbook, I noticed who wrote the beautiful, poetic words. It was my dad's sister, my very own Aunt Emma Lou Warner Thayne."

Tears rolled down my cheeks that bright afternoon as I testified that God knew me personally. Through my own relative, He created a song expressing my personal feelings and providing answers to the questions of my heart. I knew then how much God loved me. And I began to feel peace and love for myself again.

These are the serene words my sweet aunt wrote for her daughter, who had battled with mental illness years before:

Where can I turn for peace?
Where is my solace
when other sources cease to make me whole?
When with a wounded heart,
anger, or malice,
I draw myself apart, searching my soul?
Where, when my aching grows,
where, when I languish,
where, in my need to know, where can I run?
Where is the quiet hand
to calm my anguish?
Who, who can understand?
He, only One.
He answers privately,
reaches my reaching
in my Gethsemane,
Savior and Friend.
Gentle the peace he finds for my beseeching.
Constant he is and kind,
love without end.

By the end of the semester, I developed genuine love and friendship for my roommates and even the boys in our group. I felt my heart softening for them. It was as if God had taught me how to first be friends with a young man, and how not to base a relationship on physical attraction only. I was trusting again. As a young woman, I had worth to the opposite gender. I wanted to carry this healthy new perspective back to the states with me where life was still uncertain. I hoped the peace I had found in my Savior's arms would continue to support me through the difficult choices awaiting me.

It was time to go home. Even though my emotional baggage would be similar to the load I had brought with me, I was able to leave behind some unnecessary shards of punishment in the rocks of the Holy Land. The most precious and important souvenir I carried home with me—besides the authentic knotty olive wood nativity set—was a new space in my heart carved out just for the Lord, so that He might begin to heal me.

I would miss (to my surprise) hearing the Muslim prayers echoed through the streets five times a day, as well as the delicious ice cream I treasured getting on *Shabbat*, the Jewish Sabbath. But I was going home with something I hadn't had before I came: a stronger, newly woven testimony of the Savior Jesus Christ. I still felt depression buried inside me, lying dormant for a short time, but I had tasted God's reality and a seed of light had sprouted. Somewhere deep within, an unquenchable flame had been lit, linking me to a light so powerful I was drawn to it like a parched man in the desert, thirsty for more knowledge.

Dad and me (a wonderful reunion)

Israel, the night I spoke to parents about my aunt's hymn "Where Can I Turn for Peace?"

Me and my aunt, Emma Lou Warner Thayne (Recently)

Two oil paintings I crafted to remember my time in Israel.

Top: "The Garden Tomb"; **Bottom:** "An Olive Tree"

Change of Heart

"And now behold, I say unto you, my brethren, if ye have experienced a change of heart, and if ye have felt to sing the song of redeeming love, I would ask, can ye feel so now?"

~Alma 5:26

When I returned home, I felt like my world had been turned upside-down. Places and people I had been so accustomed to seemed out of place. Things that had once been important to me shifted. I underwent a personal inventory in Israel, was cleansed of the poor choices I had made in the past, and—like taking a machete to jungle thickets—had identified the poor habits I needed to change, carving new pathways for me to re-connect with God. Though it would be a long process with plenty of ups and downs, change, I decided, would start with Derrick and me.

It was our first encounter together since the long time spent apart. I could tell he wasn't too interested in the photos of Israel I'd brought to show him. He glanced at the clock, saying he needed to get back to Vegas, and leaned in for a goodbye kiss. I stopped him.

"We need to see if we have an emotional connection in addition to the physical attraction," I said. I knew this was the beginning of the end. I let the memories of us together and how off things felt decide for me then that this relationship wouldn't work out, and that it would be dead wrong to pursue a future together.

Several months later, Derrick asked if we could meet up one more time. He was ready to move on with his life, and he wanted to be sure things were over between us before he asked a woman he'd met in Las Vegas, who was widowed with three children, to marry him. As hard as it was to part ways, I knew we had crossed paths for a reason, if only to create a contrast to what I would feel when the right man came along at the right time.

Though I had assured Derrick it was over, my heart still stung when I opened his wedding announcement. I reconciled that the good woman he would marry needed his support, and I needed to prepare for the person Heavenly Father had in store for me to build a family with.

CR

As much as I loved my experience at the University of Utah, when I was in Israel I felt a tug to transfer to Brigham Young University in Provo and finish my degree. I had never claimed to be a Scriptorian, and yet I hungrily desired an increase to the spirituality I had gained in the Holy Land. I now found myself diving head first into the heart of the LDS religious world, eating up as many religion courses as I could.

I missed my dear sorority sisters from the U, but my love expanded for my new roommates, whom I had brushed shoulders with during the Israel study abroad. I began to find parts of me in these new friends I never knew existed. These were the types of girls I stayed clear of during high school because I thought they were too pure, and I wasn't worthy enough to be in their presence. In my mind, I assumed others hadn't experienced the trauma or tainted past like me, but bottom line, I did not truly comprehend the atonement of Christ and how it could heal my soul. I barely understood the abuse and its residual effects. I thought if I couldn't gel with someone else, I figured it was their problem, not mine. When I first met these innocent girls, I never thought we would be able to relate. Little did I know I would freely give them the keys required to unlock my heart, learning along the way they were similar to me, having their own sets of trials, but which came in different forms.

While at the U, I had taken mainly sports electives and dabbled in a few family relations courses, but at BYU it was psychology that held my interest. For most of my life I had been submerged in mental illness—not just my own, but my extended family's history as a whole. From my father to my brother, I was curious about how such bitter inner conflict could exist in us and where it stemmed from.

I was oddly grateful for the painstaking scenes I had witnessed not only in my struggle for discovery but also in my brave family members who paved the way before me. Many trips to the University of Utah Psych Ward were made to visit my brother Dave (17 years my senior), as he would be there months at a time. Seeing him cooped up in white prison-like walls haunted me and fueled my desire to find more than just a "holding place" for undesired behavior.

I remember long hours down in the library, sifting through index cards for research papers. It was an Indiana Jones-sized adventure into the world of brain matter and behavior. Looking back, it is crisply ironic that I would later in life be knee-deep in what I found at times to be silly discourse on the subject of human behavior. Freud, among other known scholars, pinned a good handful of odd or angsty behavior onto childhood trauma. At the time of my studies, I thought it was weak to look to the past. I was taught never to blame or trace a loss on any person or object. I was raised with the notion that medicine was the only way to tame the unwanted emotions in one's head. It was all I had known up until then, though I seemed to become resistant to prescriptions, feeling numb after being on and off anti-depressants from the time I was thirteen. Years later, however, it would be confronting my past that ultimately set me free.

I asked my mom when she began to see shifts in Dave's behavior, and she said it was not until he had a severe fever during a bout of chicken pox at the age of five. This, coupled with a bad bike accident at age 12 where he injured his head, and later in junior high when he started hanging with a not-so-noble crowd, clued me in to the possible reasons for Dave's own angsty behavior. I wondered if placing all the blame on heredity might not draw the best conclusions.

I thank my brother. I honestly feel he laid the groundwork for me in healing and recovery. If I hadn't been born where I was in our family, I might have had to walk a similar path. I am grateful Dave took the lead to live in an era when ideas, which have saved me, did not seem to be within his reach. Even though he died at the early age of 40 from an enlarged heart, due to being heavily medicated for countless years, I believe that he would have done it all over again just so I could be born at a time when alternative medicine is more respected and available. I have felt his guidance as I have pleaded with the Lord for a softer, more permanent path of healing. His memory is my strength when I want to complain how rough life can be. He fought on the front battle lines like a true hero till the end.

I had many opportunities to observe which treatments worked for family and which didn't. The problem was that we were each unique, and even as I tried the same treatments for myself, all it did was throw a wrench in the theory of medicating as a "cure all." What might have worked for another family member was proving toxic to my own body. Believe me, if there had been a magic medication that I *did not* become resistant to, I would have been singing hallelujah. But this was not my path to walk.

At the tail end of earning my degree at the Y, it was as if the Lord called me to do a field study on the effects of medicine alone without proper counseling for the buried abuse. 12 years later I would learn that confronting the trauma I experienced as a little girl would be the only way I could properly heal. A bittersweet link would form as I would reconnect with a special friend from the past for eternity, and yet in the same breath face the darkest hours yet to come.

Link 11:

Timing is Everything

"Yea, behold, I will tell you in your mind and in your heart, by the Holy Ghost, which shall come upon you and which shall dwell in your heart."
~Doctrine and Covenants 8:2

I have a theory. Some of us must marinate for a time before finding our eternal companions. The Lord knows exactly when that "right time" is, whether it be in this life or the next. If we get ourselves as spiritually, emotionally, and physically ready as we can, those individuals who are best for our circumstances will be drawn to us like butterflies to flowers. This timing is always best when left up to the Lord, who knows better than a turkey timer when the right time to pop the question is. If we marinate in His loving arms, preparing ourselves, He will bless us with happiness and bliss we could never find on our own.

While I was living in Provo, I took a trip down to St. George for a friend's wedding. There I was reunited with some friends from my short stint at Skyline High. I ran into Joe Depaix who excitedly told me his best friend Steve Ayers was returning from a two-year mission in Argentina for our church, and Joey wanted me to know about it, as he knew our paths had crossed before.

Hearing Steve's name again took me back to the first time we met:

I was 16 in Skyline's sweaty gym for a stomp. Finding me clumped in a circle of giggling girls, Alecia Thompson grabbed my arm, saying there was someone who wanted to meet me. She dragged me across the smelly, stuffy dance floor and I caught the sparkling blue eyes of this beach-blond boy whose grin alone could stop a girl mid-lip balm application. Though shy, he had this mysteriousness about him, a sense of mischief with a pinch of goodness I couldn't quite put my finger on. He was an interesting puzzle, as if so much more lay behind that killer smile. He intrigued me, though I was too prideful to admit it to myself. Back then I liked the challenge of a chase, but Steve Ayers seemed to have the whole package—looks, personality—and I felt undeserving of someone who treated me so well.

He asked me to go on a group Valentine's date with him and his friends. For some reason I drove out to Sandy to pick him up, and when I got to the door he had this silly, mischievous grin on his face and his hands were behind his back. After a heartbeat, he unveiled a darling bouquet of carnations (which are usually a funeral flower, but sweet nonetheless). I was just as naïve to gift giving, but I wanted to return the sweet gesture. I dug through the "Nedra Closet"—as my friends called the stash of freebie stuff Mom collected in case she needed a last minute gift—and found a sample bottle of Ralph Lauren cologne. Steve later told me how nice he thought that was, and how he kept it for years.

Steve also remembers an awkward time from high school when he came over to my house for a visit, and I asked him if he wanted to see some of my art and poetry. As I read to him from the most private part of my soul, he listened intently and patiently. Although I wrote this experience off as time passed, Steve kept it in his heart, claiming later it was more intimate than a kiss.

Our relationship was sporadic when I transferred to Rowland Hall. We got caught up in our own high school friendships and athletic worlds, Steve with football and me with tennis. I remember a time when I heard a girl mention his name in passing as I walked down Rowland's halls. She can't go out with him, I thought, an unjustified jealousy surging through me. It was strange, since at the time I wasn't interested in furthering our relationship, yet something inside me hung on to the connection we had forged as friends.

‍‍ CR

At the wedding of our mutual friends Jen and Tyler Wilkinson, Joey's mention of Steve piqued my interest. When I drove back to Provo, I mentioned Steve to my friend Amy Iverson, who had known him longer than I had as she had attended Skyline as well. "Do you think you could set something up for us to meet again?" I asked her. Amy was the Ayer's greatest ally, having already set up Steve's younger brother Joe with his wife-to-be, Trina Derby, who was also in Gamma Xi with me. Sure enough, one Sunday night Amy and Greg, her hubby, invited the both of us to their condo in Murray for dinner and games.

Now, the other returned missionaries I had dated usually came back after two years paler and skinnier than ever, but when Steve walked in, my eyes went wide. He was tan and lean and muscled, the result of bicycling through the mountainous Argentine terrain. He looked like a statue of a Greek god, like *David* by Michelangelo. His nickname back in high school was "Smiley" because of his deep dimples, but it didn't do him justice. He was utterly jaw dropping.

The photo albums I had been looking at before he arrived were forgotten, and I was about to get up to give him a welcome back hug when something struck me to *play it cool*. I couldn't be one of those many girls I was sure were falling all over him. I was not playing games; I just didn't want to look desperate. If you hear this story from Steve's perspective, he will say I could have been friendlier after two-plus years of not having seen him. At the very least I could have given him more than a nod and a "What's up?"

In spite of the awkward reunion, Steve stirred up the courage to ask me out. We dated for a while, but when the word "marriage" came up, I froze. Things had just ended with Derrick that same year, and I reasoned there would be nothing more awful than another goose chase led by emotions alone and not God's approving hand. Knowing Steve had volunteered to help his sister Nancy Cozzens, a former Miss Utah, with pageants by escorting contestants off the stage, I didn't feel he was ready to know if I was the One or not, when there were other girls to meet. So I suggested that he gain a little more dating experience before we got too serious. His heart seemed restless, and I wanted to be in a situation where we both felt confident about our direction. For several months we dated other people, but then one weekend in late September of '94 everything changed.

My sweet Israel roomie, Shauna Hall, and her posse up in Sandy were taking a trip down to Lake Powell and they invited me. We called up Steve and his older brother Len to join us, as we needed a big group to cover the costs. I did not count on them coming because they had committed once before to come on a trip to Yuba with a few of us but were a no show. I still had strong feelings for him, but I was not going to bank on them while he was still tending to that field of young ladies.

Shauna called me last minute to switch up the driving arrangements. To my surprise, she said, "Hurry up! Steve called, and he'll be picking you up shortly!" I assumed he would be just one of many people I'd be carpooling with, so I did not think much of it. That is, until my roommate ran into my room and with bated breath said, "Peg, there is the *hottest* guy here to pick you up, and he is ALONE."

Be cool, I reminded myself. Not wanting to risk reading into something that was not meant to be, I moseyed on out as if Steve was a brother and not a *boy of interest*. Yes, I admitted he looked yummy, but I was not about to run straight into uncertain territory again. I wanted the Lord to guide the voyage in order for me feel at peace knowing He saw the end from the beginning. I had learned my lesson when it came to forcing a decision on the Lord He already knew was not in anyone's best interest.

The car weaved through narrow, red rock canyons, and at every pit-stop I had to pinch myself, a reminder that Steve was "just a friend," and to just play it cool. I felt my emotions pressing on me. Having arrived at Lake Powell's loading docks ahead of the rest of our group, we decided naps in the sun sounded like a good idea. I remember pulling out my scriptures and praying with all my might not to fall for a possible false connection with this irresistible hunk sitting next to me, but to instead build a wonderful friendship. And that's exactly what happened.

Whenever my feelings for Steve swelled like the wakes of the boats, I would train my focus on another friend in the group who had asked me out prior to the trip, pretending that he caught my interest. I was attempting to not let on to my intensifying emotions. The timing had been wrong before, so I was in denial over the possibility that Steve could be my ever after.

The girls in our crowd of 25 caught on to Steve's charm. He was a hot commodity, and I prided myself for being so levelheaded. Many times we would separate for volleyball games or boat runs, but as night fell in, Steve and I seemed to find our way back to each other like the waves hugging up against the bank of the cove we were nestled in as a group.

We went on a dirt bike ride together, and after many glances and shared smiles, I knew I was falling deeply "in like" with him regardless of my attempts to play it safe. We did not kiss that trip, and I was true to my guns, but when it was time to arrange the carpool for home, I found myself excited to ride together alone. One of his admirers would be joining us, however, making up some silly excuse why she needed to ride in our car, like attempting to make it back home for her church service because her ride told her they would be a couple hours behind us. A little miffed, I tried not to let it get to me and bit my tongue as her ride followed us almost bumper to bumper all the way north to Provo, leaking her real intent of making her move on Steve.

Nevertheless, even before we pulled onto the road, Steve reached over and gently took my hand, holding it the whole way back to Courtside Apartments, where I lived. Something happened in that moment. Steve was a pretty shy guy, and for him to use PDA in front of another girl was serious. We had grown closer. And even though I was nervous that the other girl would make her move after he had dropped me off, a feeling of ease soon replaced it. The Lord's timing was perfect. He was filling me with faith and reassurance that if it was meant to be, not even a silly, giddy girl could block the road.

Within a week's time Steve called and I had him over for a homemade meal. My cute friend Shauna Cleverly helped me conjure up. I was extremely nervous, not being a good cook. Steve was so kind and patient with me. As I went to put a tinfoil-wrapped baked potato in the microwave, he gently called out, "Wait, Peggy, I think you need to take that off before it cooks, to prevent a fire..." Embarrassed as ever, I removed the foil, but I also felt that this might foreshadow of a home life together. I am notorious for distractedly walking away from meals and burning them, so this felt comforting knowing he had my back.

After several months of dating, Steve would join me for Sunday dinners with my family up in Salt Lake. One evening he casually leaned over and said to me, "I could see us having many more dinners like this one." An unfamiliar calm filled me as I looked at him. I knew what he was implying, and I finally felt heaven confirming that he was the one. The miracle is that it didn't need to be a lightning strike, only a feeling of peace in my heart. A link of love and peace was filling up the dark corners of my heart, but would it hold to the altar?

Steve Ayers

Link 12:

Steve: My Eternal Companion

"Did I not speak peace to your mind concerning the matter?
What greater witness can you have than from God?"
~Doctrine and Covenants 6:23

Come October, it was time for my apartment contract at Court Side Apartments in Provo to either be extended for another semester or sold. I called Steve, who will tell you that I shocked him when I bluntly asked, "To sell or not to sell...this is the question? I finally have a person interested in buying."

He paused for a quick moment and then responded, "Sell it!" as if we were on the floor of the Trade Center making the biggest investment of our lives so far. To this day, I still get butterflies thinking about it! The pieces were falling quickly into place—almost too quickly for both our comfort zones.

Steve's family was living up by the Bountiful Temple at the time. We made many trips up the hill to look out over the Great Salt Lake and went four wheeling in his white Toyota pickup. Steve was really into Rugby his senior year in high school. After his mission he and another best friend, Tim Smith, played for an adult Skyline team. I cheered him on through many tournaments. If there was one thing that made me giddy it was watching him play eight man and flanker (aggressive positions in the sport). He was later picked out of many other players to play on the Western Conference team. Steve's talent to run like a deer and get into a "ruck," as they call it, was heart stopping.

Hanging out with his family and having Sunday game nights with them was a blast. I loved how competitive we were. Steve was winning my heart, and I knew I was ready to seal the deal. He was the seventh child like me, but of eight children, rather, in eleven years (bless his mother's heart!). I would gain a whole new set of sisters and brothers whom I gelled with seamlessly until later when I would take out my pain on them as well.

I will never forget the day Steve called to report he had asked my parents for my hand in marriage. He assumed my dad would be the hardest to convince, but it was my mom who quizzed him until he felt dizzy. After an hour of grilling, Mom finally saw what I did in the man I loved, and she gave her approval for this "gentle giant"—as she phrased it.

On Christmas Eve when Steve came to pick me up for his family's festivities, he presented me with a dozen red, long-stemmed roses. As I put my nose to the flowers, I figured something was up. Turns out he was playing the False Alarm trick! We'd already picked out a ring, but Steve conveniently told me it wouldn't be ready for several more days. I fell for it!

A few hours later, Steve's family put on their traditional Christmas pageant for all of us. As the wise men (played by Steve's nephews) walked up to the baby Jesus to present their gifts, one of them (darling Bronson) stopped in front of me and handed me a little white box with a bow on top. I heard some family members call out, "Okay, Steve!" and he dropped to his knees.

Steve, in his Prince Charming-type humility, looked up at me with the most heartfelt expression and asked, "Peggy, will you marry me?"

Totally caught off guard, all I could say was, "You little liar!" when I meant to call him "sneaky." Laughing and wiping the tears from my eyes, I gave him a soft but solid "Yes." Later, I told him it was a keen move on his part to ask in front of his whole family, as a part of me felt gun-shy to leap into this territory again. Even though I loved him, fears of the past crept up like old water marks from a high tide.

Unlike with Derrick, I had prayed about marrying Steve back in October, asking if it was right before we got into serious territory with the family. The memory of a sweet, soft confirmation where God whispered, "Yes, Peggy. Steve is eternity," made my answer roll off my lips. I believe the Lord reserved Steve and me for each other, and, through our individual challenges, prepared us for marriage. Our relationship was built on a foundation of faith, as well as a healthy friendship that later grew into a romance so enduring not even the riptides of abuse could sever our bond.

In addition, I had a tradition where I usually took someone I liked to play tennis to see if they could pass the "good sportsmanship" challenge. I wasn't that great of a player, but sports tell a lot about someone's attitude, and because it was so important to my family to be a good sport, I was silently weeding out the poor sports caught up in their ego. The first rally I played with Steve, on the same courts I'd played on with Dad and Ned, wasn't until we were engaged—which tells me how much I internally trusted and loved him. Even though he swung the racket more like a baseball bat and hit the ball three courts over, I found everything about him irresistible. He was such a gentleman and could care less if he was making a fool out of himself—at least we were doing it together.

◌

After our marriage in the Salt Lake Temple on a cold February morning in 1995, life felt like the night sky with each star lined up in perfect order. I was on the occasional dose of Prozac, but like before I would go off periodically, as I didn't like to feel medicated even if it meant sinking low.

90

Steve worked for a while with his older brother Leonard and brother-in-law, Kary, installing cable lines, while at the same time finishing his finance degree at the University of Utah. I was teaching tennis to youth groups at the Kearns Recreation Center and the Murray Sports Mall. The first months of our marriage were bliss. Heavenly Father knew we would need this firm foundation for the rocky terrain ahead.

Many summer nights were spent out on our 3rd floor patio, looking out over Murray Park where fireworks went off in the sky and in our hearts. Spontaneous flowers, sentimental notes left in each other's cars after work—love could not have felt more seamless than this.

After nine months, Steve and I felt we wanted children. But three years went by with no luck. We were both tested. Except for my endometriosis that required periodic laparoscopies to manage, we should have been capable of getting pregnant. I was on a five-year plan at BYU to finish my degree, and it was not until the last semester, last class, that it finally happened. Steve and I were ecstatic! Until our excitement slammed on the breaks when I went to the doctor's to check on the baby's heartbeat.

Because I was only eight weeks along, I was sent to the first floor of the hospital for an ultrasound. The ultrasound technician took extra time searching for that tiny heartbeat, and my worry increased with each passing second it was missing. She casually looked at me and said, "Ma'am, you need to go back upstairs to schedule a D and C. There is no baby." Her tone was effortless and as routine as if what she were really saying was, "Go fetch the milk out of the milk box before it spoils."

That walk back up to the doctor's office was one of the loneliest walks of my life. Heartbroken, I felt that my body was rejecting a baby and, with it, my dream of becoming a mother. When I told Steve, he was equally crushed. Having grown up in a family with eight children, he was so eager for us to start building our family. He assured me that this wasn't the end for us; we'd keep trying.

The following Tuesday, I had the D and C (which is a procedure to remove tissue to clear the uterine lining after a miscarriage) and we thought, *Okay, we'll try again in a few months.* For some reason, by Saturday I was growing weaker and sicker. I was throwing up and could not keep fluids down. We rushed to the ER at St. Mark's Hospital in Salt Lake City. Over the course of 5½ hours, 16 attempts were made to draw blood. I was severely dehydrated, and the technician said my tests were reading that I was still pregnant. She went back and forth, contemplating my results. She was sure the D and C went well, but could not figure out what was causing my pregnancy count—which shot from 800 to 1500 within 3 days, indicating something growing—to climb.

My OB came in and told me how perplexed everyone was. Either I had a tubular pregnancy, which meant there was an additional baby growing in my fallopian tubes besides the one they had cleared out of my uterus just days prior, or I had something called a molar pregnancy. In any case, I would have to be admitted to the hospital to be treated.

When a nurse came in with a huge needle in her hand, I said, "No way. The doctor promised me no more needles!" I was traumatized from getting so many pokes! My OB quickly came in to explain to me how serious a molar pregnancy was, and that it was a matter of life or death. I had no choice but to listen carefully and take every treatment she gave me. She told me a "molar" is a type of pregnancy where too many male chromosomes form in the womb, mimicking a baby through blood tests. It is actually a form of cancer, and was rapidly multiplying in my body.

Looking back with current eyes, I honestly wonder if my body was shutting off the areas where the abuse had occurred, creating another hypothesis of why I could not conceive. I know not everyone who has been abused faces issues like this, but in my case I believe my body was manifesting a resistance or backlash for the trauma it had experienced. It had had enough!

I knew this was a time I needed to seek out my Heavenly Father more than ever to calm my troubled heart. He succored me through my sweet husband. Steve took the best care of me, even helping me finish school. I had only one paper left to write to graduate with my degree in psychology, but I felt too exhausted to finish. I was ready to throw in the towel when Steve offered to type the paper as I dictated it to him. Actions like these were simply Steve's nature. How blessed I felt to have married a man who loved me beyond my physical and mental abilities! God truly knew Steve would deliver when I could not.

When my will was His, Heavenly Father had cleared this unique pathway for me to marry the man who would be my rock when I felt like crumbling, and who created a safe place for me to finally let down those protective walls I had left standing for so long. The effect would benefit the both of us for eternity. Luckily we would not know what was in store for us when the blissful newlywed dust settled and the door was opened to a crazy mix of emotions and heartache.

For the next six months I had to have monthly chemo shots. After four months, I had hoped that my will to have a healthy baby would overpower my body's illness. It was not that easy. I underwent several laparoscopies to scrape out additional endometriosis, and I needed to have cysts removed on my ovaries every couple of months. I refused to listen to my body, brushing off my pain as trapped gas. Once, I got up in the middle of the night to work out on my treadmill. I pressed my stomach against it as I walked, hoping to rub away the stabbing in my abdomen, a pain similar to barbed wire. I was determined to fight against the fact that my body was rejecting any chance of bearing children.

Sadly, I remember an experience I had with a counselor, shortly after returning from Israel, where I shared with him my hopes of getting married and having children. Without warning, he said, "You don't want to pass on those mental illness genes to your children." Though his words cut to the bone, making me feel like I was damaged goods (which, deep down, I knew was completely ludicrous and only his opinion) I could see his point. I had felt resentment towards my parents for passing down the so-called "depression gene" (which I learned about from studying textbooks and my family's history), so it made sense for me to break that cycle. My stomach tightened as I realized I wouldn't want to create mental heartaches for my children whom I would dearly love. When I thought about the abuse I had suffered, I froze at the idea of the same type of harm and torment coming to my own children. All these arguments made sense to me logically, but not emotionally.

I still wanted children with all my heart. I longed to connect with these kindred souls tracing back to the subtle voice of comfort I felt influencing me in the Holy Land.

Links that were building me up now felt like they were snapping. The role of motherhood which I had wanted ever since my days of nurturing my doll Suzanne now looked so distant and out of reach. Who would have known that five years into my marriage with the spouse of my dreams, I'd be facing the unanswered question of why we couldn't create a family?

Steve's family throwing me a bridal shower;
also, his five beautiful sisters (upper right)
singing at our wedding breakfast

Steve and I were married on February 25, 1995 in the Salt Lake City, Utah temple

Our first year married!

Link 13:

Divine Connections with Birthmothers

"I can do things you cannot, you can do things I cannot; together we can do great things."

~Mother Teresa

Shortly after our heartbreaking news, Steve and I were visiting my parents' home ward for church when we ran into a doctor who was just leaving the foyer. My parents introduced us, and we told him about our struggles and some solutions we were considering. Then he made the most profound statement, as if straight from Heaven. He said, "By the time you spend thousands of dollars on in-vitro fertilization or other avenues, trying to have a child biologically, you could already have two or more children if you were to choose instead to adopt."

Astonished, Steve and I looked at each other, and our hearts were filled with a comforting Spirit. We knew this was the route we should move forward with, while still trying to naturally bare children as well, but who knew? Maybe they would come to us both ways. All that really mattered for us was to receive the special spirits God would send regardless of them looking like cookie cutter molds of us. We just wanted to be parents, regardless of how our children landed in our arms. Further comfort and confirmation came over me as we moved forward in faith, recalling the tender moment in Israel where I had felt the gentle influence of my children nudging me from Heaven. I knew their time to come to Earth was almost here.

Steve and I jumped on the opportunity to adopt as if it were second nature. The process was exciting and nerve-wracking. Each step was like leaping from lily pad to lily pad. Back then in 1997, I handcrafted our birthmother letters. Looking at pictures of families on the computer today and seeing how adorable they all look, I am amazed I had the confidence to send mine. But the truth is I felt divinely led as I wrote, and even in choosing the type of paper to print the letters on. I would later learn from one of our birthmothers that calla lilies were her favorite flower, and that by printing her letter on calla lily stationary she felt an additional connection to us.

How do you start a letter to a mother who is already in turmoil? Honestly, I had to plead, one desperate mother to another. There was no room for fluff. I had to put my heart into each word, promising these mothers that Steve and I would be the parents they were searching for to raise their children. As much as I hoped and wished that my words would penetrate their hearts, though, I was not naïve. After hearing the birthmothers' stories of how they chose us, I knew we were simply a small part of a larger miracle. I believe the Lord can create masterpieces out of any dilemma, broken hearts and all.

If you ask anyone who has walked in the way of the adoption process or foster program, they will tell you it is a "risky heart business," because you put every part of your heart on the line—from excitement to rejection. We had so many loved ones warning us to play it safe, to not get our hopes up; but to the tell you the truth, you just have to jump in with both feet. You cannot exactly play it cool as you attempt to stay cautiously optimistic. If you do not bear your heart to these two sweet angels—both mother and child—you might come off as indifferent or uncaring. Steve and I felt like our whole existences had culminated up to the point of our union and becoming a mommy and daddy to these precious spirits. We were willing to show the vulnerability it took to finally have our children in our arms.

Next to the Savior Jesus Christ and His infinite Atonement, I believe there is no greater sacrifice than a parent setting aside her will for the best interests of her child (in my eyes, at least). Each time after bringing our babies home, we felt the ache and anguish of the birthmothers. What must they have gone through to make the decision to let their children go? A birthmother and friend of mine explained it to me this say:

Peggy, to know you just trusted your infant to a family hoping they love her the way you would and knowing [she is] still on this earth is a pain indescribable, but at the same moment you know you did what God wanted you to do.

Sometimes I wonder if it would have been easier to have lost my child  *and to have the knowledge that she is safe in Heavenly Father's arms. To trust another family with the sacred task of raising my little girl in this world was truly the ultimate test of obedience and sacrifice. To have seen the beauty and potential of my little girl and know she wouldn't be coming home to me was excruciatingly painful, but the undeniable confirmation that I received gave me a wave of peace amidst the heartaches I was facing. I knew she was a daughter of God who had to come through me to find her family. I love her more than anything and that is why I knew she deserved more than I could give her.*

~Katherine DeSantis

(used with permission)

We could not promise our children's birthmothers perfection, but we could promise them that their sacrifice would never be in vain. With each breath of praise, we would utter their names. The links of faith and hope would try our hearts as we longed to connect to a birth family. Only time would tell if we would receive a call to become parents.

Luke & Grace:
Literal Lifesavers

"Jesus took the little children and blessed them."

~3 Nephi 17:21

Gratefully, not too long after we submitted all of the lengthy paperwork and attended the potential parent classes we were required to take (which, by the way, should be mandatory for all parents, as they really help couples see how they will raise their children while at the same time getting them to talk about diaper selection!), we received our first call to meet up with a birthmother. Steve and I were cautiously optimistic. We were invited to go interview at her brother's home in Sandy. It was a cloudy day, but even a tornado could not have swept away our joy. As her three-year-old daughter danced and twirled around the room, Joyce asked us a number of questions about how we would raise her son if we were given the opportunity. I knew if we were to be chosen that Luke (the name we would later choose) would be just as adorable and energetic as his older sister.

It might have sounded premature, but as Steve and I left the interview I said to him, "This is the baby boy we have been waiting for." With tears in his eyes, Steve agreed wholeheartedly. Sure enough, the call came that Joyce had picked us after many prayers and carefully deciding between three possible families. She had three months to go before giving birth, so Steven and I had plenty of time to create a nursery. Joyce was so kind as to give us his ultrasound photo, which we hung on our fridge and kissed and prayed over throughout the day. Luke had settled in our hearts long before he would grace our arms. This was the most beautiful possibility we could have imagined. It didn't matter if he wouldn't look like us or not; his heart was ours.

Joyce went into false labor once, and our longing to hold Luke in our arms grew like no other desire we had ever experienced as a couple. We prayed often to our Heavenly Father to keep our son safe as Joyce began to feel emotionally threatened by the birthfather, who wanted to keep the baby. The morning we received the call that Luke was arriving felt like Christmas. Our nest was ready to bring our little bird home to. We loaded up the backseat of our car with gifts for our newborn and his mother, and set off to meet our son.

I was blessed to have been invited to witness his birth. The little guy fought so hard! They had to unwind the umbilical cord not once but three times from around his neck, but he came out on top and he was healthy. High emotions filled the delivery room as Joyce's name was listed under "Code Red" (meaning she was given a false name) in order to protect her and Luke from the birthfather. Still, Joyce was able to foster a sense of peace. She exchanged Luke back and forth seven times with me. Each time I held him I felt guilty, but she kept encouraging me, wanting me to bond with our son. It was a moment when the heavens opened, and together two mothers shared the joy and heartache all wrapped up in one, while grandparents and an anxious new father waited in the hall to meet our new "Lukey."

Was he beautiful? Words cannot describe the miracle of having a baby placed in the arms of longing parents who were told they would likely never bear children. But God knew us and He knew our son. He knew this little soul was ours regardless of whether I could bear him myself or not.

Joyce was amazing. She gave us our own room as if I had borne Luke myself. The nurses kept coming in and out, reminding us that Joyce could change her mind at any time, so not to get too attached, and also that any medical decisions concerning Luke were not ours to make. Not three minutes later, the nurses returned, embarrassed to say that Joyce had confirmed Luke as ours. I could see Joyce's heart wear down as she passed her precious baby boy over to another family after nine months of mothering. She would be like a loving aunt who would occasionally come with her brother and his wife to see how Luke was doing, giving an angelic response—like only angels can— that he was breathtaking. Joyce was truly one of our earthly our angels.

☙

Learning how to change diapers and run for days on minimum sleep would prove to be the least of our issues with bringing this miracle boy home. The custody battle between the birth father and us lasted three very long years. He had fathered eight other children and never put up a fuss before. Although I am sure he loved Luke, most of the tug-of-war seemed to be between him and Joyce for control, though that is simple speculation. He had made some poor choices, but we all have worth in God's eyes, and he was just as important to God as any of us, just maybe a bit lost at the time all of this took place.

Most of our nights were sleepless. Although illogical, a desperate feeling to flee the country with our son, should the state award the father full rights, consumed our thoughts. Thankfully, God granted Steve and me a blanket of peace. If I sat quietly enough, calming my fears, the Spirit would reassure me that, although the time being would feel desolate, our son would soon be ours for eternity. We just had to be patient and have faith that Heavenly Father would take care of our hearts regardless of our questions of the unknown.

At the close of one of the hearings as we were exiting the court house, with all the muster of a mother who would stand in front of a moving truck to save our son, I said to the birthfather, "You will never have our son. Never!" Tears rushed down my cheeks. I knew I had crossed a line, but our faith was unshaken. Luke was ours. Finally, the judge asked the hard-hitting questions to the birthfather, and the case closed in our favor.

◌੪

Between Luke and our future daughter Grace, we had a birth-mom choose us and then pull out the day of placement. We were crushed. We hoped he would be ours; we had even chosen the name Jonah for him, the name of the boy in *Sleepless in Seattle*, one of my favorite movies. It was a tough next few weeks, to say the least.

Needing a distraction, we took a trip to Disneyland, where we spent a good portion of the next three days in our hotel room crying on the bathroom floor. The loss we felt was similar to what we had experienced during the molar pregnancy—which felt like a death. Even though I had had a feeling the birthmother had not truly connected to us, it still hurt. Yet even in our despair, the Spirit whispered peace to our hearts, reminding us of the bigger plan ahead.

On our return trip, we received a call from our adoption agent. We had not even left the airport yet and here we were getting the happy news that we had been chosen by another birthmother. This time, however, we recognized the feeling of uncertainty and graciously passed. We felt that this particular child was meant for another family. As odd as this may seem, we know we made the right choice, for not even three weeks later we received another call about a birthmother who felt strongly we were the couple for her baby.

Jeannette, our future birthmother, had reviewed the profiles and was considering another family when she said she had a dream about our family adopting her daughter. She quickly called the agent overlooking our case, expressing assurance that her daughter was meant for our family.

When we heard this, we knew another angel had come into our lives. We were so grateful and eager to meet our sweet, selfless Jeannette and soon-to-be little Grace—a name so sacred to me, as it was my middle name and my father's mother's name as well. We just knew she would be called Grace from that first spark of hope!

As with Luke, we went to the hospital to cheer on Jeannette when it was time for Grace to come into the world. Right before the final push, Jeannette asked one of her best friends if she would leave the room so I could come in and see Grace be born. Touched by both women's selflessness, this again was a sacred experience I cherish with all my heart.

While visiting over the next couple of days, Jeannette shared a scared moment with me that I will forever hold close to my heart. She told me her dad was not sold on the idea of her placing her baby for adoption, as it can create a hole in the entire family's heart, not just the birthmothers. But then he walked into the waiting room and saw who Grace's potential adopted grandparents would be, recognizing my father Gill Warner as a man who had once come into the service station where he worked. Most of the customers who came in were stuffy and condescending, but he said my dad treated him with kindness and equality. After realizing where Grace would grow up, Jeanette's father gave her his blessing.

How grateful I am for a father who not only affected another man's life for good, but who was able to plant a seed of trust in his tender heart. Would the adoption have proceeded without the wonderful connection between two fathers? Maybe, but it was more meaningful for Heavenly Father to have created this special connection long before our paths crossed—even before I was born. My father came to mean that much more to me, and his dedication to be

Christlike no matter where he was in life became a legacy to me. This lesson is worthy of emulation because we never know when we can provide solace in a critical situation—or simply because it is the right thing to do. My mom's example of love complemented my dad's. It is true that behind every great man is a supportive wife. Together they laid a firm foundation I have been able to rely upon countless times linking me to blessings.

Having my dad seal (which is the highest saving ordinance performed in LDS temples) Luke and (six months later) Grace to Steve and me for time and all eternity in the Salt Lake temple was worth all the heartache it took to arrive at that point. I do not believe we really understood the magnitude of how sacred these two events were. The road to feeling the security of these two beautiful babies sealed to us at times was unbearable, rough, and tearful. Yet in that space of becoming an eternal family, all bitterness was transformed into a tranquil symphony of peace. Steve and I have often thanked our Heavenly Father for the obstacles we had to climb over to reach the top of those precious moments, because the reward of never giving up is more glorious than having blessings easily handed to us.

I know we each suffer differently, but I promise you, I would quickly give up not having stretch marks on my stomach for the knowledge that the child in my arms is ours and will never be taken away from us. In the same breath, I realize that the temple ordinances are just the beginnings of staying together forever. We relished those sweet moments in the sealing room, for truly our hearts were linked as one forever.

Not for years to come, when hormones and residue from the past crept into my life like morning glories, would I truly realize the magnitude of these two miracles. They would be the lifesavers I would hold onto when the thought of going on felt impossible. When I think of that little nudge in Jerusalem to get my act together and trust the

Lord with my life, I also think of the two spirits waiting to come down, who did not yet have the mortal veil clouding their eternal viewpoints. They knew Steve would be the companion who would stay by my side through the tornadoes of life, and they knew they would give me a greater reason to hold on when the effects of abuse roared with full vengeance. Sometimes it takes loving something more than yourself to hold on. Our children were that something.

Families

Are

Forever!

Left: Luke
age 8

Bottom:
Grace age 7

Luke and his selfless birth-mom, Joyce, plus family

Grace and her creative birth-mom, Jeanette, plus family

Link 16:

"Teaching Days"

"And it must needs be that the devil should tempt the children of men, or they could not be agents unto themselves; for if they never should have bitter they could not know the sweet."
~Doctrine and Covenants 29:39

Despite the joyful experiences I had with Steve and our children, I was still sinking deeper and deeper into depression. I think I am like most people when I am in the middle of a trial. At the time, I cannot see the purpose for my pain. But now I have learned to see that everything has a purpose, which makes those bleak moments somewhat tolerable. I like to call these my "teaching days."

Soon after Luke's custody ordeal was finalized, we lost my niece Heidi in a horrific car accident, just two years after losing Dave, her father. She and I were extremely close. She, too, had been sexually abused, though as a preteen. I was with her when she was taken to Primary Children's Hospital to be examined. I remember so vividly Pam asking the hospital staff why the boy who had done this to her daughter wasn't also going through the same explicit examination.

The boy had lured Heidi in at a party and verbally broken her down, convincing her that she had no other choice. Heidi knew it wasn't her fault, yet, like abuse can do, it made her feel dirty as if *she* had done the wrong, not her perpetrator. She fell into a deep darkness. Her clothes changed from fun, light colors to dreary shades of black. Her hair and her image were altered, as if she were trying to cry out for help as I did through my tantrums as a toddler and my disobedience as a teen.

Heidi was one of the sweetest, most caring girls who might have agreed to a journey as rough and prickly as her father's. They were kindred spirits. Just a week before she was killed in a tragic car accident at age 19, Pam found her cuddled up with some of Dave's belongings, expressing how much she missed him. Like her daddy, I feel she was also welcomed home, embraced in the Savior's loving arms.

Losing Heidi was like losing another sibling, and I felt my emotional load had hit its limit. Steve and I thought that uprooting our family and trying to establish ourselves in a warm, memorable place like Santa Clara, some three miles outside of St. George, might help lift  my spirits. Unfortunately, they were lower than ever. My problems seemed to endlessly follow me around after the newness of the house and neighbors wore off, though no offense to either; they were just a temporary distraction for my pent up emotions, ready to erupt if not properly addressed.

Luke and I (I'm backtracking a bit; Grace would be adopted about a year later) would walk the landscapes almost daily. He turned two and was out for adventure. Luke was my everything, yet my body wouldn't do what my heart longed for. I was determined to be the mother he deserved, and I think for the most part when I felt well enough I was. If it had only required willpower, I would have wished my depression away for my child's sake. The guilt of being a vacant parent, even though I was physically there, was crushing and sunk me into an abysmal despair. I once heard someone equate depression as "a living coma," and it is. The eyes may be open but your mind is a thousand miles away. My negative thoughts multiplied: *Oh, Steve and Luke would be better off with a wife and mother who can do what I should be able to do. This isn't fair to them, or to me.*

Ashley and Amy visited me once in the Red Rock Valley. I remember barely caring if they came or went. I was numb to feeling any joy or happiness, which was odd for me because I am usually a person who thrives on company. With the scorching summer heat keeping us inside, about the only thing I could do to find joy was eat. My weight skyrocketed and the snowball effect was massive, attracting all sorts of debris as I morphed into a Peggy I had never known before. It was beyond discouraging.

I recall a hot afternoon when I had stayed home from church because my depression and anxiety felt more unbearable than the desert heat. I tossed and turned in my bed, wondering if and when this grief would ever lift. I remember calling out to God to help or just to end it all. Though I never attempted to take my life, I was on the brink. The Lord knew I needed help, and in that last watch, He delivered. I called the local hospital and told them I was as desperate as a person could get and didn't think I could hang on any longer. This was the first of six voluntary visits to various psych wards.

My first visit to the St. George psych ward was interesting. It wasn't like the doctors or nurses were mean; rather, I just felt hopeless, as if I had been diagnosed with a disease and cattle-branded like I was as a child, poked and prodded by university psychologists. I could not explain to them why the feeling to end it all came on like a swarm of bees ready to sting me for getting too close to their hive. Because I had asked for help, I was now placed in a bleak white room, left alone to somehow find solace, yet was truly in a morgue of nothingness. I felt like a menace to society but had committed no crime. Though I realize these places and medication can be great outlets for many people, I was again playing the victim.

I missed my family upstate and felt more alone being away from them, even though it was *my* rash idea to move in the first place. I was running from family issues that weren't the real problems. *I* was the problem. My husband was doing his best—*more* than to be expected, in fact, working two jobs and then playing nurse to me in my dark hours. I would dread him leaving, feeling the darkness take over not only the night sky but my heart as well. The silence was awful. Worse, my self-sacrificing husband had no clue how to help me, yet he gave me every ounce of what he could and then some.

Sadly, the one friend I did find a connection with and tried contacting outside the walls of the psych ward was told we were not allowed to have contact with one another. We were instructed to sever all ties, as our friendship might spark unhealthy thinking. Here, finally, was one person I could relate to (though she had later gone the full distance in ending her life), but I couldn't reach out to her. Even more alone, I sat staring at my prison walls. The gorgeous red hills I had found so much peace and adventure in as a teen became a backdrop outside my bedroom window of how trapped I felt. Not even the past memories of working out in those hills as a teen could spark a glimpse of hope.

☙

We lived in St. George just six short months then moved our little family to West Jordan, desperate for the support of our extended family we had once thought of as an obstacle. I remember how modest, but lovely, our home was—newly built in a community called Ivory Highlands. It was quaint, but lacking the serenity I was hoping for—as if a new zip code could change the sending address to my nightmares. Over time the image of the house morphed in my mind into a homeless shelter with dirty walls and rough floorboards. This time of my life multiplied with bleakness.

I matriculated from psychiatrist to psychiatrist hoping one of them would know the right combination of prescription drugs to eliminate the war zone in my head of thoughts like *I'm not good enough to be a mother, wife or daughter*. I was so determined to defeat the darkness that I followed the psychiatrists' instructions almost to a fault. My medication tracking charts were impeccable— Sunday at noon, Monday at 7 a.m., Tuesday at 10—I almost never missed a day. I never wanted to be found sitting in their offices reporting that I had not given a hundred and ten percent. If there was a perfect combination of medications to help me, I was going turn over every rock possible. Like the trained athlete I had been in the past who learned never to give up, this, too, would be an opponent I would not walk away from, no matter how many matches challenged me.

One counselor I met with at the advice of a psychiatrist introduced me to a huge package of behavioral vocabulary definitions. Intriguing me, I felt like I was back at the Y, fishing through index cards for my next psych paper, but this time I was the subject of investigation. It was like getting the screenplay on how inept characters functioned on the stage of life, and the spotlight was on me. I was discovering myself in all of these unwanted behaviors. It didn't seem to resolve anything, only magnify how crazy I felt. The proof was flashed in big lights every time I acted out.

Once when my close girlfriends and I were away on our yearly, girls-only trip (to remind us that we were more than housecleaners), I took a whole stack of laminated cards so that I could study all of the different unhealthy brain patterns I was manifesting, such as "blaming" or "catastrophizing." I was determined to cut off those negative behaviors. I probably drove Julie and Amy nuts. They learned more about psychology than they ever wanted to know!

Between my prescription cocktails and thyroid imbalance (which threw off my hormones) and in addition to having a hysterectomy at the early age of 28, I continued to gain weight. As hard as I would try to run or speed-walk the 5-mile perimeter of the community park, I couldn't lose a pound. It felt like someone had placed me in a scuba suit with weights sinking me into the pavement. Unable to resist the near-magnetic pull, I spent more time eating and sleeping. No longer could I just go out and burn off lunch or dinner like I could as a teen. My shadow of weight engulfed me, countering how I coped for what I felt inside. I was a glove being pulled inside out. My outside finally reflected my inside battle.

My self-esteem plummeted. I no longer felt like a spunky, trained athlete or an officer in a society where I made a difference, just plain, old, ordinary Peggy who tended to repel people with her dark bubble of sadness and anger of protection. I had not yet discovered that having those labels of being "champion" or "officer" were only a façade making up a respected identity that did not really matter. As we know, image is just a mirage after all.

I felt continuously judged because I didn't have the close proximity of the people who had known me through my growing up years when I had been in prime shape. Fortunately, my college friends were a constant in my life regardless of the ugly vibes I was giving off, both physically and emotionally. My cute friend Julie would drive forty-five minutes from Draper to meet me at the local gym where she would personally take time with me to train me on weights, like we did in college together, and be my cheerleader when I would want to give up on the cardio machines. And all this out of the pure love of her heart. Other times she would encourage us to go play tennis over at our local park to find that missing Peggy she knew was still in there.

Then she'd take me to the store and show me how to pick out healthier products so I could attempt to slim down.

Ashley and Amy were ever so kind to come visit me occasionally from out of town, and kept in contact via phone when they could. I had true angels who loved me and gave me a spark of connection to the real me, even if it was to hear their voices.

For one Christmas Steve bought me a plane ticket to fly up to Washington and spend some time with Amy. She toured me around like a queen of the city, shopping, eating at the Seattle Space Needle, and spending time on a ferryboat. But the most fun of all these was to go to the movies together like we loved to do when she lived in Salt Lake. In my alone time with Amy I would link to that place where the raw me was. She, too, loved me regardless of my weight, status, or even the mood I was in. At the time, I did not see the full sacrifices my friends and family were making on my behalf, but years later I am deeply appreciative of the love of each one.

CR

West Jordan brought with it my angry and frustrated years when I was questioning everything in life—even my faith. I remember sitting in Relief Society at church one Sunday, and the poor teacher got the question of the year. I asked, "What if you're not sure that what you are teaching is true?" Rose Hutchinson, the Relief Society instructor, was so sensitive and patient. The expression on her face was full of love and sympathy; it said, *Peggy, let's chat after. I can tell you're in pain.* She called me later that day and gave me some verses to read in the Book of Mormon. Rose saw through my prickly countenance and knew I was not so much questioning her gospel lesson as I was questioning if God really knew I was alive. It didn't feel like it. The chains I was carrying around were crushing every ounce of hope, which I was ever so desperate for. When you're in the teaching days, it feels like a maze with sky-high bushes blocking the light needed to find the path to a way out.

One morning I was on the phone with my mom and I told her I didn't know if I could hold on in this state much longer. Unbeknownst to me, she had called 911 on the other line, as she lived 25 minutes away and felt I needed help immediately to stay safe. There I was in my living room with my young children as they ran in and out, carefree and happy, and I saw the paramedics pull up to the curb. I wanted to "flee from the crime scene," so to speak. I wasn't really going to hurt myself. I simply needed a respite for the dark feelings. Bless my mother's heart for trying to save her child, but I was mortified. In that moment of desperation, I never thought to physically hurt myself; I just wanted the self-defeating dialogue in my head to stop.

Mrs. Haberlie, one of my selfless neighbors who lived up the street, happened to be walking by and asked if she could watch my children for a little while—truly a Godsend, but now my secret was out about how truly crazy I felt inside. I was a mentally screwed up parent who could not hack the laundry of the day. I was humiliated that everyone in the neighborhood would know how dysfunctional I was. My pretend walls I lived behind were falling for everyone to witness.

I was back in a psych ward, the only place at the time I felt that could hold my frequent episodes of desperation. At least I could be somewhere that mimicked the loneliness of my heart. At mealtimes it felt like the patients were paraded for all the visitors to see how dysfunctional we were, though I am sure it was just my own insecurities bleeding out and not what was really going on. Where was the girl on the tennis court, rallying with her opponent, now? Had that life been an illusion or was this negative space I was in the counterfeit life? I had no clue why the thought to end my life kept rearing its ugly head.

Rarely did the memories of the doctor abusing me surface, and at the time I would have never linked it to my acting out. Only the coping mechanisms, like over-shopping or spending days in bed, were magnified. I considered bringing up the abuse in group therapy, if only because it had never properly been addressed, but instead all my blame fell on the people I wrongly felt did not love me. It was weakness to me when others in the group therapy referred to their childhoods. I clung to the belief that it was petty to blame past events, and I was still unsure if what happened to me really happened because it was hardly talked about as a child. Pep talks about how to not blame a lost match on a racquet or an opponent seeped into this area as well blocking any view of seeing what was truly fueling my unquenchable fire.

We tend to connect to people who seem to "get" us, if only because misery loves company. I remember a nice fellow during my third psych ward stay at Valley Mental Health in Midvale. At this time my husband seemed to be the crux of all my issues. As kind and selfless as he was in my mind, it was easier to look outwardly than at the reflection in the mirror. *If only he could understand my problems better*, I thought. This dram of toxin spread like wild fire. Straightway, this new friend advised me to distance myself from him, pointing out all the negatives I had mentioned in group therapy. Sadly, I listened and acted on the misguided, slanted advice of someone as off as my judgment was, which only created a worse space for Steve and me. He was lonely and frightened, but at the time all I cared about was me, the victim.

Poor Steve, here he was each night after a long, hard day at work, bringing the kids in with him to see their mommy, and all I wanted was for him to leave. If I was going to be jumping down a hole of misery then anyone in my proximity needed to prove their love by jumping in with me. I honestly can't believe he came back each night.

I was vicious! I would lash out at him as if all my problems stemmed from our strained marriage. I had *voluntarily* placed myself in all six psych wards, and yet I was throwing daggers at anyone who was living the life I longed to live. I wanted my babies, but somehow couldn't love them the way I dreamed of as a child. Seeing Steve and them during visiting hours felt like salt on my gaping wounds. Here was this beautiful family within reach, but I had no strength physically or mentally to embrace it. My vision was temporarily clouded and delusional, so I couldn't recognize the supportive spouse I was blessed to be married to in these bleak moments, regrettably using him as a beat-up-stick instead.

Except for those doses of medicine deep enough to put you into REM, nights were horrible. I dreaded sleep more than being awake because it seemed that all the what-ifs had box seats in my psyche. At least during the day I could keep them at bay with how bleak and distracting my slippers looked in my closet of at maximum three items allowed; or with the activities we did as groups, such as painting flower pots, which were only later reminders of how dysfunctional I was when I saw them in my kitchen windows at home.

Back at home, I felt I was not only in the mental cage abuse had placed me in as a young child, but now my external my walls coincided with my inner walls. The raging bull within could not be contained any longer. I was a menace to my family and myself, and I felt absolutely hopeless. People saw me as manipulative with a cruel tongue when I felt threatened, which wasn't too far off. When you are so desperate to alleviate the pain you may have adult tantrums, say offensive things, and lash out at anyone unable to understand your pain as you do.

I am sure my sweet children struggled during this time, wondering why I was either emotionally checked out with them or was literally gone and when I would return. When we were home, I would muster up every last inch of energy I could to play games, teach them, and snuggle. At this time, Luke was around seven and Grace was four. Sometimes they visited Steve's sweet parents who lived a close six minutes from us or we would go visit my parents for the afternoon. While I slept they would play in grandma's famous toy drawer in the kitchen.

On summer afternoons when I could hardly function at all, we opted for a daycare program at a kind woman's home down the street. Because I had been a nanny in college and saw how much those children longed for their mom, not me, it killed me to drop my kids off at another caregiver. My children needed me and I needed them, but my body was barely hanging onto its molecules of strength. They needed to feel peace in mommy's arms, but love wasn't enough to fuel my energy. If I regret any part of my life and wished for a do-over, this part is it. However, I have to believe that if I truly feel I agreed to this journey, then my children, too, saw what lay ahead for them as I did. This may not be fair, but I've had to trust that they also have connections to be forged with their Savior through trials, and my lack of presence provided a branch to reach out to Him.

In addition, I found myself getting into arguments with my in-laws over petty things. Mixing two backgrounds pushed my opinions to extremes, so that I did not make for good conversation. I had fallen in love with this family at the beginning of my marriage, and now I couldn't handle being at an Ayer's family event without feeling explosive. Almost everything they said felt like a literal dig into my fragile, almost nonexistent self-esteem. By finding fault in my family members, I seemed to have been proving to them how unlovable I was. In my mind, no one could understand me, and I felt the victim of abuse within my own family, the people I served with in church callings, and even my closest friends. I was my worst enemy, sabotaging any sign of a healthy relationship.

If there was an S.O.S. sign for someone drowning emotionally, it might include some of the aspects listed above. If we truly knew how to unravel the ugliness, I promise you, most people struggling would have found hope by now. It's ugly, uncomfortable, and exhausting to be around those struggling for rest in a constant battle to want to hold on when the goggles they are looking through are so muddied.

As I denied my feelings, I began to fight the toughest opponent I ever had to face: the *will* to fight off the deepening depression. As most victims do, I felt guilty for the abuse on some level, even if it wasn't forefront in my mind. I directed constant negativity inward and hammered my fragile mind with self-doubt. Although I was young, I lost confidence and the ability to see any value in myself, and started down the lonely road of self-hatred and inner turmoil. I tried to convince myself that if I just ignored my depressed feelings, like in tennis, the match would soon be over, and everything would be okay. But it didn't work that way. I thought that the whole world was out to get me and that I was *linked forever as the victim.*

The West
Jordan
years
~
Hard times,
but good
friends!

Link 17:

The Last Thread of Hope

"Now when our hearts were depressed, and we were about to turn back, behold the Lord comforted us, and said: ...bear with patience thine afflictions and I will give unto you success."

~Alma 26:27

So many times I thought that truly the world would be better off without me. My husband could remarry the wonderful, healthy woman he deserved and my children could have the functioning mother I promised their precious birth-moms. My parents and other family members wouldn't have to fork out mounds of money to compensate for my hospital bills and shopping sprees, which seemed to give me a flicker of relief from the darkness looming at my door. It is incredible what your brain believes simply because something is forefront in your thoughts. The endless game of fighting off self-destructive thoughts is tiring. For this purpose I am grateful for the respite periods in the wards, even if they were only a Band-Aid over the real problem.

At one point, my doctor prescribed a cocktail of prescriptions, including Adderall (an amphetamine and a relative to meth) along with a number of emotional stabilizers, including an anti-anxiety medication to compensate for my uncontrollable highs. I would have 90 minutes of happiness as I climbed to a massive high, only to fall into the grips of a suicidal pit. The drugs were fueling the crucible inside me.

At a time when depression seemed to dominate my daily life in spite of my desperate search to find relief, I found myself returning to the psych ward for the fourth time. As prosperous as it seemed, the first time I sat in on the support groups I was astonished. I listened to the heartfelt stories of other patients who had attempted suicide but were revived; they lamented because they were still on this earth. I was beginning to understand how haunting it could be to hold on when despair seemed to be the only emotion I could feel.

The original stamp of rejection and worthlessness the abuse had given me kindled my suicidal feelings, though I didn't recognize it. But despite the nagging thought to give everything up, my will to live strove for solutions. After exhausting all of the usual treatments, I was approached by one of my doctors who suggested I try electroshock therapy.

ECT is used to treat severe depression when medication has been rendered ineffective (called refractory depression). When explaining it to us, the doctor used an analogy of a computer. When the computer malfunctions or stops working, a common solution is to shut it down and reboot it. Essentially the same effect could be obtained by sending low-level electric shocks to the brain.

Having already had a son undergo the same treatment, my parents were familiar with it and hopeful that it would help me as it had appeared to help Dave. I, on the other hand, had no clue what to expect, or even if it would work. Still, I dove in, ready to try almost anything in order to return to my role as a "normal" (if there is a true normal) functioning mother and wife.

What did I have to lose? I felt defeated, it did not seem like anything could make it worse. Being the non-quitter I was, and holding on simply for the fact that I did not want my children to ever have a reason to give up in their lives because of my example, I agreed. I had a feeling it would not be effective for my body and mind, yet I felt like I was out of options. Medicines may have provided a tourniquet to stop the flood of constant bleeding, but it was as if I was a hemophiliac, and the depression was an uncontrollable bleeder.

The night before my first treatment I lay in my bed in the psych ward, numbed and slightly delirious from the heavy medications. Around three in the morning I was startled by a man in white scrubs entering the room with a large needle, which he injected into my thigh. It was a shot to dry up my saliva prior to treatment. He looked like someone coming from the morgue to roll my lifeless body away, and to this day the memory is vivid in my mind, affecting my sleep.

In the treatment room, I was eased into a Lazy Boy recliner and left to wait for the inevitable pinch of the saliva-drying shot from the orderly dressed in white. I couldn't help but feel like I was waiting for the electric chair on Death Row. My father and Steve were there on every occasion, but no matter how often I looked to them for comfort I knew I would be walking the next 45 minutes alone. My arms were strapped down and I was hooked to an IV feeding an anesthetic so I wouldn't feel my body's spasm-reactions as my brain was being rebooted.

When I closed my eyes, the sedation taking hold, who knows where my mind would go. Though disturbing for him to recollect, Steve says the doctor would place a damp sponge (which helped conduct the electric current) on my head and secure it with a cap. Electrodes were hooked onto the cap, and a bite guard would be placed in my mouth to prevent me from biting down or swallowing my tongue. The doctor placed his finger inside my fisted hand to measure my reactions, as I would squeeze it while the ECT was going. The electroshock itself lasted only about ten seconds, after which I was unhooked and allowed to come out of the anesthetic.

I remember waking up and feeling as though I had just run a marathon with 100 pound weights strapped to my body. The two doctors gently called my name, calling me back from outer space, but it was Steve's loving voice and my dad's kind touch on my hand that kept me from disappearing into a black hole for eternity.

I finished about five complete treatments while in the hospital and then stopped, as it was not showing progressive results. Upon my sixth committal to the psych ward, no one could figure out why I was so despondent. Doctors urged me to try the shock therapy one more time. Again I thought, *What is there to lose?* I already felt defeated on so many levels. They explained that the more shock treatments you do close together in a row, the more powerful the results would be in attempting to reboot the brain out of a stuck state of depression. This only made me feel more defective, as nothing—not even the most extreme of treatments—could alleviate my issues. My self-worth was as broken as the attempts to fix me were.

The longing to give back my husband and children their original wife and mother I felt was locked inside me somewhere compelled me to each appointment. Loving someone more than myself helped me push through the many thoughts of giving up.

A close relative who had heard of my dire straits phoned me one afternoon. He had worn the child's shoes of looking into his mother's bedroom and wondering if she would make it another day. He asked me point blank if my children had ever heard me talk about giving up.

"Yes," I replied. "Just the other day they walked by my room and heard my cries to Steve that I didn't feel I could go on."

He then proceeded to let me know how this felt to him when he was a child. He told me to commit to him right then and there and make the same promise to my children.

I repeated back what he said to me and later to my children. I promised: "Mommy will never leave you and she won't ever give up!" They were not to worry anymore and could feel safe knowing I had made a commitment to them. Making this pact with them helped me sift through the moments of hell, even if it was simply to keep a promise to persons I treasured more than leaving the all-encompassing darkness of my mind.

This is not to say those who have lost the battle to suicide did not love their families. No, my point in sharing is to reach out to those who feel there is no reason left to hold on. There is ALWAYS a reason—whether you believe it or not! One of my favorite quotes encourages, "Don't believe everything you think," because sometimes what we feel is farther from the truth, and those whom we believe would be better off without us would actually be hurt the worst.

We stayed at my parents' home the night before my next ECT treatment. My children were downstairs, sleeping safely with their grandma and unaware of their mother rising at 3:00 a.m. to go the hospital. Dad and Steve, my anchors and escorts, were by my side as I pushed through the hospital doors with all the faith and courage of a soldier going off to war, praying to survive the front lines of insanity. The sterile smell of the hallways made me cringe as we trudged our way to the second floor. Steve and I looked at each other, a mustard seed of hope between us that this time we would see new results by sticking it out longer.

I dreaded the nauseous, numbing state I was about to walk into, which had been one of the reasons I stopped the treatments in the first place, yet I didn't trust myself to say enough is enough when my life looked so bleak. I knew I was dragging my soul into a nightmare, but because it was being recommended by a doctor with a degree, somehow, I reasoned, it should be okay. I would go out on a limb to say this mimicked the feeling of being forced to go to a certain place I despised, but not by my parents this time, by my so-called sentence to live a mentally ill life. I did not mean to see through the eyes of a victim; I just felt trapped with no visible door.

After each treatment my body was spent. The male nurse and Steve lifted me into a wheelchair to be taken to the car. The brisk air at 5:30 a.m. reminded me of the mornings spent with Dad and Ned at the tennis club; however, now I was bound in a lethargic state of defeat and hopelessness. If I could make it home without puking, it would be a miracle. Steve would carry me through the house, past our children who had awakened at the sound of a turning doorknob.

"Mommy's okay," I'd mumble to them. "I'm just going to go sleep for a bit." Then my dedicated mom would try to entertain them with a book and breakfast.

Snuggling back into bed was about the only reward. I would sleep for hours, rolling around with the headaches that could last for 48 hours or more. I groaned as my children jumped on the bed, needing the attention their distressed mother was unable to give—but not for a lack of love or desire for them. The shock therapy took energy I did not even have in reserve.

Thoughts of doing this all over again in less than a week felt like insanity to say the least, but if I was going down I would go down knowing I had given it my all. When the doctors asked me if I saw improvements, I am sure being numb resembled some sort of relief. Truthfully, though, it only kept the defeating thoughts at bay for so long. All the vivid darkness of how depressing life felt returned like a boomerang. I had now done a total of 16 sessions of ECT, and my body finally screamed those words "enough is enough." Loved ones around me could see the lack of progress, and we all retreated like a defeated army with only gumption in our hearts to push us forward.

I will never know how the shock treatments really affected my body and mind. To this day, flashbacks of the treatments haunt me, and I continue to struggle with associated fears. I cannot downplay the vital role these treatments played in the lives of other depression survivors. And perhaps they saved my life in some ways, too, if only to help me realize how blessed I was to have loved ones waking in the wee hours of the night to serve me.

In these moments, seeing through the victim's eyes is what I needed to experience in order to one day link to others in the same awful desperation. This was the course God was asking me to walk through. In these moments I held onto a flicker of hope for a new healing. I would have loved not having to go through my hardest years, but the ripple effect of the lessons those years taught was invaluable to the Lord's eternal plan for me. I would not go back and change a thing. This does not mean I pray to the Lord, saying, "Pile on the trials!" But I do pray for humility. I pray to be able to submit my will to His in order to make sense of the senseless.

The key links to uncovering the truth behind this madness would soon come as a whisper to my heart when I would see a painting of someone who had suffered like me. It would say: "There is one physician whom you haven't yet turned to, He is the Master of troubled hearts."

Link 18:

The Master Physician

"But if ye will turn to the Lord with full purpose of heart, and put your trust in him, and serve him with all diligence of mind, if ye do this, he will, according to his own will and pleasure, deliver you out of bondage." ~Mosiah 7: 33

After ECT therapy proved to be unsuccessful once again, I did not have many other options. There were some very heavy psych meds I had not tried, but inside I knew prescriptions were not the right avenue for lasting relief. Concerned, my family urged me to give it just one last shot. I was warned gaining more weight was a possibility, and I had to have frequent blood tests to make sure my body was not reacting adversely to medication. I was getting further away from myself. At this point, I felt that I had only two options left: either leap off a metaphorical cliff or find a way around it. I urgently needed to find my new method of relief. I was certain that if this medication failed, God would have to intervene.

I thought that with the discipline I had gained as an athlete, I could keep my past from dictating my present. I didn't realize the depression was related to the abuse. I thought I should be able to control my negative thoughts and feelings. I thought with the knowledge from my psychology degree, I could suppress the feeling that I was somehow worthless, damaged goods. But now when the shock treatments failed, I shifted my focus back to what I had known since I was just thirteen: prescription drugs.

After only two days and terrible reactions to the medication, I felt little hope. I kissed my children goodnight and tucked them in, drained of the strength required to last another day. Even though I promised them I would never give up, I felt I just couldn't ward off the heaviness any longer. Steve held me close, pleading with me to hold on. He knew that my will to live was stronger than my desire to die. He promised me the world. He would quit his job, stay home and take care of me until we could figure out a cure for my sorrows. "I'll never give up on you," he said. I knew he meant it. I also knew that this trial was a test of faith. No matter how long the pain lasted, I needed to believe that, according to God's plan of eternal happiness, my sorrows would be but a small moment.

I knew there was more to life than numbness and simply existing, but my beliefs in my own willpower failed me. I was non-functional. I had a nanny care for my children and a housecleaner. (This is the fairytale portion of my story, as I realize that not everyone who suffers has this type of help.) Steve dealt with almost everything while I was in bed most of the time. The depression finally hit its limit. If one of the best psychiatrists in Utah and most powerful electric shock treatments couldn't bring light to my darkness, then there was only one other source out there I hadn't turned to yet. It was time I sought a new physician.

One Sunday in church, after a particularly hard week, I saw the painting of the woman reaching out to touch the Savior's hem, based on a story from the New Testament of the bible. It tells of a woman with an "issue of blood" no physician could cure her of (Luke 8:43). When Christ was out among the people with his disciples, she saw him passing and thought, "If I may but touch his garment, I shall be whole" (Matthew 9:21). As I studied the painting, I felt that this woman must have been as desperate as I was, searching twelve years for lasting healing from a terrible disease. She had so much faith that she knew by simply touching the hem of Christ's robe, she would be immediately healed. And she *was,* for Christ said unto her, "Daughter, be of good comfort: thy faith hath made thee whole" (Luke 8:48).

This was the moment when the whisper of peace overcame me so distinctly, prompting me to turn to the master of troubled hearts. I decided to open my heart as this faithful woman had. As soon as I could, I fell to my knees and asked for direction like I had never done before. Right then I realized that in my heart I *knew* God loved me and would help me find true peace, but I didn't know when or how it would happen. I thought I may even have to wait until I saw Him face to face, but I knew I would be made whole. I longed for His healing now, though, because I knew that my two young children (now ages ten and seven) needed me.

Later that week I asked for a Priesthood blessing (which we believe is the authority and power to act in the name of God) from a man I greatly admired. I knew this church leader was hesitant to promise me anything, but he assured me that it was truly up to our Father in Heaven and His will for my future. Fortunately, he felt that this was the will of the Lord, and that in time I would step onto the road of recovery with new doctors who thought outside the typical "medical-box." Because I had tried Western medicine without yielding much of a return, my eyes were more than welcome to a new vantage point. He also let me know God loved me and was aware of me. He would guide me to new methods of healing, but I had to keep up my faith while being open minded and put in hours to find results.

∞

My pathway to healing was only just beginning. I was advised to meet up with a German holistic healer in Bountiful who helped me discover I had Epstein-Barr, which is a virus that causes the lymph nodes to swell, inducing fevers, and can lead to mononucleosis. Long, long days were spent being poked and prodded to determine why my body was on the fritz. After she diagnosed me with Epstein-Barr, I was put on an interventionist treatment plan. Twice over a period of three weeks I had to get ports put into my arms—which unfortunately created two blood clots which had to be removed—so I wouldn't have to get poked numerous times a day (finding a vein has always been difficult).

My soul lit up when the healer told me I might have been misdiagnosed all these years. At the time I was on nine emotional medications, not thinking of how to safely come off them. I made a very thoughtless move. I was so eager to be free once and for all that I went cold turkey off of four of them. When my body started to go into fits of withdrawal, twitching uncontrollably, the healer kept a closer eye on me.

I was so grateful to be getting a new kind of help that I did not complain much at first. But what I had done was unlock a Pandora's box of sealed off emotions pent up for three decades. Not only did my body show signs of malfunction, but my emotions were at the height of extremes. The lows were so low it felt like spiders were crawling all over my nerves, trying to escape. The headaches were unbearable. One night she had Steve and me stay after all the other patients had left to inject over 25 shots into my scalp to try to relieve the pressure. It was unsuccessful, but we all get A's for trying—me bearing the pain, her for not giving up on attempting to alleviate the pain, and Steve for being so patient and willing to never give up. In addition, my family members and kind neighbors also did their best in looking after my children.

One day in particular she kept watch—unbeknownst to me—because she was afraid I was having a stroke. She could not quite put it together, though, because my body wasn't showing all the symptoms of a stroke. Finally when we chatted late that night I confessed that I had come off some of my meds on my own, as I was so excited to be rid of them after she told me I was way over medicated; my body was just plain worn down. I was going through major withdrawals, but by the time I happened to mention what I had carelessly done the repercussions were already in full force.

My parents were in shock. My mom could not bear to watch my body contort. The German healer assured her that it would be cruel to make me backtrack; I was almost through the worst of the withdrawals, and to go back on medication would hinder my efforts at detox and in finding new healing.

I remember getting on my knees in her quaint little bathroom after three consecutive weeks of sometimes eight to ten-hour days of B-vitamin shots and constant liquids running through my weak veins, in an attempt to counter the virus, simply pleading with the Lord to stop the needles and pokes even if she meant well. My pained body triggered back to the time of the molar pregnancy with the countless needles. I just wanted it all to stop.

I seemed worse off than when I walked through the door the first day. She was not trained to deal with the emotional side of illness, but she sure gave it a good shot. During the day she would have me sit a comfy chair with headphones on and try this new light therapy she had recently purchased. It was like trying to taste an ice-cream cone *without* taste buds, as the dominating thoughts of anxiety and darkness smothered any sort of attempt to find joy.

Two incredible miracles did happen, however, while attending this cute and spunky holistic healer's clinic. After weeks of pleading to God to make the needles go away once and for all, I was pulled into her office. "Peggy," she remarked with fervor, "other physicians would not believe your levels if they saw your test results. It is truly a miracle. I have patients who have been here for over a year now continuing to battle the same ailment, but your Epstein-Barr has gone dormant." What she meant is that my test results showed that the virus was retreating. A feeling of peace and reassurance that the Lord was listening cloaked all my anxieties. I still needed to take care of myself, being careful not to overexert myself and bring out the virus again, but for now I was on the mend.

The other miracle happened one night in our attempts to quiet my body. Going cold turkey without proper permission and supervision had been a bad move on my part. Days went by and my withdrawals didn't seem to be lessening. One night as Steve came to pick me up after my daily dose of nourishment, the healer decided to try a new approach. Most of the staff had packed up, leaving just the three of us. She took me back to a new room where she had thousands of dollars' worth of medical equipment. She, Steve, and I put on ultra-protective goggles to protect our eyes from the red light therapy she was going to use to attempt to calm my convulsing body. Ten, fifteen, then twenty minutes went by without progress, though not due to a lack of her committed efforts, trying every tool she could think of. My body simply was not responding to medical science.

She took off her gloves, pulled down her mask, and asked me if I wanted Steve to give me a Priesthood blessing. To be honest, the twitching did not really hurt as much as it looked. After weeks of shots and shock treatments from years past, this felt like just an annoying tick preventing me from breathing smoothly, as my neck would jolt to the right every 15 seconds. I looked like a robot shorting out after getting splashed with liquid.

My faith was weak and I was exhausted from the day's efforts, but I saw her faith. I turned to Steve and nodded. "I guess it couldn't hurt."

Steve, with what energy he could muster up after playing both mom and dad at home (plus putting in full days at the office so we wouldn't lose our home and could pay the mounting hospital bills), gently placed his sweet, strong hands on my head and asked the Lord to calm my troubled body. By the second sentence his voice spoke, my entire body from head to toe ceased to move, like watching a person come out of a seizure. The room was filled with the Spirit, and no one spoke for a few minutes. The holistic healer took off the rest of her gown and goggles and simply looked up at both of us. She said, "Well, Peggy, we know who the true physician is. God's healing power trumps all the machines money can buy. He is truly our loving Heavenly Father who is aware of our cries for help."

My work was not over that day. It took another five years to uncover the beast that lay dormant behind all the medicines for so many years.

I was taught that if I ever had a glimmer of doubt if God was real and aware of me, I had only to remember that sacred night when not even the top instruments were powerful enough to calm my troubled body, only God's gentle blessings. With the Lord as my captain, I could trust that I would one day be led to further healing. Slowly but surely, links to heaven were being forged. As I did my part, God would keep His promises and I would see glimmers of distant hope.

Link 19:

New Eyes

"Trust in the Lord with all thine heart,
and lean not unto thine own understandings."
~Proverbs 3:5

Not much longer after that night of comfort, the German healer called her associate in Provo, asking her to take over. She felt she had done all she could do for me and that it was time for me to be looked at with new eyes. She assured me I would be in safe hands, yet I felt mixed emotions. Hers was the only road to a fresh start I had been exposed to thus far, but I knew we had hit a dead end when it came to my emotional needs. So, I followed her suggestion and we set up a meeting with Dr. Morrison.

It was a Saturday. Her weekday schedule was booked, yet she was selfless enough to meet with us. We had the whole office to ourselves. After giving her the lowdown on the remaining medications I was taking (as that seemed protocol with all the other doctors we had seen the first time), I committed that I would be safe and not go cold turkey again on any medications.

Then she asked me this question: "Peggy, could there be any other reason for your pain—an accident, trauma, or anything you haven't dealt with?"

A little stunned, I replied, "Yes, but long ago.... It's in the past." I nonchalantly mentioned I had been molested by my pediatrician and knew it had happened but that's that. As an athlete in the Warner home, I was taught never to blame or complain about anyone or anything, so this seemed logical.

As Dr. Morrison and Steve went over my medication list, she told me to go wait out in the foyer, but to do one favor for her. "As strange as it may seem," she said, "when stress arises, try telling the little girl inside of you she can walk out of his office at any moment." Honestly, I thought she might be kookier than I felt. But I was open to at least trying, as I had made a promise in my attempts to find true healing to never give up and think outside the box.

Out in her foyer alone, I tried it silently to myself. I repeated: "Peggy, you can leave at any time. Just go!" Though I said it halfheartedly and with a smirk, I was shocked at how it created a space in my tight chest for me to breathe.

That day marked one of hundreds, practicing mantras under her care as I learned, for the next five years, how to unlock the chains my little girl had been shackled in for three decades now.

How could something so simple work so powerfully? We had been told by someone else who saw results from her work that our family's viewpoint of mental illness would shift as we learned how she helped us see with new eyes what truly healed the soul.

Dr. Morrison had me get a notebook and for the next six months write all the negative thoughts that came into my brain. At night my subconscious worrier had the front row to throw popcorn at any chance of peace and sleep, but now it was being drawn out—welcomed even—onto a huge pad of paper. It was like a valve had been loosened, releasing all those trapped, nightmarish realities I had never faced until this point in my life. I would sit with Dr. Morrison in her office and read her pages upon pages of excruciating emotions that had surfaced from memories of the abuse, and how I felt about my family not acknowledging it the way I desired for validation. She knew so keenly that in order for me to let the light in I had to first empty out the secret closets of my heart, layer upon layer.

Like most good treatment plans, results were slow. My faith was wavering as I faced a new level of uncovering my emotions. I learned abuse is as toxic as cancer, and that with the combination of medications, side effects, and withdrawals on top of it, my senses were confused and reality was not clear to me for quite a while.

I had an experience one day when I was ready to cash in my chips that proved this to me. I had just met with Dr. Morrison and was choosing to slowly come off some more of my medicines. I stopped at my parents for the afternoon, depressed and anxious as a result of immediate withdrawals. Desperate and triggered by the past, I opened their medicine cabinet. Even though I was seeing subtle results, the dark hours still felt unbearable. Knowing an overdose was not going to help and was far from rational thought, I suddenly stopped and pulled myself into their TV room. There I dropped to my knees and pleaded once again to know if Heavenly Father was really there.

My parents had a Book of Mormon on their coffee table. Needing strength, I randomly opened to a beautiful passage near the beginning where Nephi (one of the ancient prophet's discussed in the book) asks to know if what his father Lehi (also a prophet) saw concerning the destruction of their city Jerusalem was true. Because Nephi's faith was unwavering, he was shown everything he desired. Lying there, I wondered if I could be as strong and faithful in my conviction if God was there for me. Yes, I had a beautiful patriarchal blessing to know I was on the right track, yet I needed a solo connection with my own testimony to truly see me through the rough hours of withdrawals and facing the ugly past.

I cried out to Heavenly Father to at least let me know He was there, breaking the chains I was tangled in to set me free. I believed that, even though I felt lower than dirt, God would hear my plea as He had the prophets in the Book of Mormon—not because I was deserving; no, simply because I was His daughter.

I prayed earnestly to know He would be my side through this ordeal. I even attempted to express gratitude for my trials and the horrible feelings I was having, which was one of the tactics Dr. Morrison had taught me in order to combat defeating thoughts when they arose.

I didn't hear a voice, but a wonderful feeling came over me that God *did* care! There was a quiet stillness urging me to go home and to trust that comfort, and that genuine healing would come in time. I felt His love teaching me the great news of the gospel, which is that our Savior's atonement covers all of life's experiences, not only sin, turning trials into testimonies of His divine connection with us.

I went home and, as I had in the past, cuddled my children to remember two of many precious reasons for holding on when the dark seemed to paralyze me.

Later that night, I had the most amazing dream. I was in my Savior's arms, completely dead weight. My head and limbs were hanging down as if I were already lifeless. He was carrying me and walking slowly. I had on a gown with holes in it, and His brilliantly white robes gleamed through them. The peace was as exquisite as His robe's whiteness. I knew that only *through* His grace could I truly have that inner peace, and that I didn't need to die to feel it as I had previously believed in moments of despair. He had always been there for me and always would be as I faced life's difficult challenges if I simply had faith in His love and His atoning power.

I awoke with the most joyous feeling I have ever experienced in my entire life. I removed myself from my child's bed. Looking for a piece of paper, I found the back of a bill to write down what happened to me that night so I would always remember. Soon after, I realized that the holes in my gown were a representation of Christ's healing of the trials—or holes—in my life. Although the memory has faded more than I wished, I know without a shadow of a doubt that on this special night I was given the witness that our Savior is more REAL than anything in this life. I found myself thinking that I didn't want to spend time on frivolous projects or accumulating things that don't really count if I can't take them to Heaven. I also learned that He *literally* carries us when we are alone and feeling worthless.

I was given a taste of heaven to help pacify the desolate moments to come. My healing didn't take place in that instant, like the woman reaching out for Christ's hem. Rather, I believe the Lord wanted me to be able to help others moving forward, and the best way to do this was for me to know hardship in first person while learning the methods which lead to freedom.

When I sought after my psychology degree in college I had wanted to either be a motivational speaker or someday be a social worker. I decided that night of my dream that if Christ was showing me He had been there all this time, especially in those moments when I felt so desolate, then I could face *any* path He needed me to walk down to help others. My attitude shifted as I had a peaceful place to return to when fog overcame my thoughts while in the process of healing. I knew nothing was going to keep me from repaying Him for giving me the glimpse of heaven as He had that night.

A drawing my daughter Grace drew up
for me after I told her about my precious
dream!

Alternative Methods of Healing

"Draw near unto me and I will draw near unto you;
seek me diligently and ye shall find me; ask, and ye shall
receive; knock, and it shall be opened unto you."
~Doctrine and Covenants 88:63

To assist my stubborn brainwaves that seemed to get stuck in obsessive thinking—and also to help my anxiety and depression—Dr. Morrison set me up with many sessions of neurofeedback, using an EEG machine which measured my brain waves to produce a signal which she could use to interpret my brain activity. Although it is widely used and advertised as an alternative way of healing without side effects, back in 2009 it was just a way to break through some tough mental roadblocks. After producing a thorough brain scan, Dr. Morrison was able to know which areas of my brain were out of balance.

A technician of hers would come to my house two or three times a week and set up a computer which had my data and personal treatment plan logged in so the electrodes could properly read which areas needed to be retrained, as they fed information back to the computer. For example, my Beta waves were extremely high, creating lots of anxiety, so this is the area we started with first. Completely different from ECT, the electrodes would simply read my Beta wave lengths, transmit the information to the computer, and then the movie I had chosen to watch would pause until the desired wavelength was found. It was fascinating because I would not have to do much other than choose a film I liked (though not a violent one) and sit back for 30 minutes as the machine worked its magic. The brain is so smart that it *wants* to watch the next scene in the movie, and it will do whatever it takes to make this happen, thus creating a reward system for the waves to perform the desired data entered.

Within a few treatments I noticed subtle differences, such as not reacting so drastically to a situation that would have put me in a total meltdown like before. Dr. Morrison explained it like learning the piano or a new language. It takes time to create new pathways. I had trained my brain subconsciously to overreact (as a result of the trauma as a child and forming unhealthy coping methods) and would feel that the world was coming to an end, when simply it had been a stressful day. Retraining my brainwaves with the combination of facing fears that threw them out of whack in the first place provided a permanent place of healing for both the emotional and physiological parts of my brain. I needed both to truly find a way back to before the events all took place.

In addition, I also learned that the reasons I could not commit to work or people and why I struggled to be a functioning adult in my marriage and parenthood was due to the fact that we sometimes get stuck in the age of the trauma; if not healed properly, our emotional growth could be stunted. In times that caused me stress I would revert back into that little girl, making it necessary for me to go back to those trauma moments and re-teach her—as *adult* Peggy—what was really going on, helping me find the trigger I needed to heal and mature.

Making sense of why I had been acting out all these years was incredibly liberating. I did not care if I had to drive all the way down to Provo in a handcart (as I lived 45 minutes away)—this was working! But most importantly it was *sticking*, unlike other treatments that fell short in the past. There are not words in the human vocabulary for the gratitude and excitement I felt as we saw results after results, uncovering the real me piece by piece. My family was also starting to see little glimmers of their true daughter, wife, and mom—it was truly a miracle!

Dr. Morrison and her staff bent over backwards for me, as they did for many other patients, and with the guidance of God worked miracles with me for the next five years. She has since moved on to a new city to treat new patients, but I will never forget her unwavering efforts to help uncover the root cause of my issues. I love her with all my heart and pray she may know I am forever indebted to her as a kindred spirit in the medical field. After three decades of searching, I felt so blessed to have been led by God to the healers who were His conduit in finding resources to heal. The miracles we experienced together as we both put God at the helm of my healing process were priceless.

ॐ

Within the same clinic I also met a fabulous healer named Cheri Harris, who works under several doctors in Utah County. She is not a counselor, as she says, but has learned how to help physical and emotional stress find a pathway to true healing (under doctor supervision, of course).

She helped me with allergy treatments first and then later moved into other areas Dr. Morrison asked her to assist me with. Going on six years now, I still have weekly visits with Cheri, yet it is usually on the phone because I am not in as dire straits as I used to be. Together we uncovered many layers of residual effects the abuse left behind which needed special attention layer by layer. She is blunt and honest with me yet in the same breath tender, non-judgmental, and sincerely empathetic in validating my pain—an excellent platform for healing.

I call Cheri my "exfoliator" because her work and inspiration guides me in lifting the crusty, unwanted, and self-limiting behavior from the past. As simple and non-invasive as this seems, days later I felt the efforts of her powerful techniques continually releasing the trapped emotions in my psyche. Her methods are not harsh, and assist with lasting healing from the past.

I learned through counseling with both Cheri and Dr. Morrison that the abuse had powerfully affected my young and pliable mind. It created wrongful beliefs about me and the world which snowballed and attracted debris, seemingly confirming them. This is typical of what an abused person experiences. Looking back, I see how the abuse resurfaced with various relationships, as I sometimes tried to hurt those who wanted a close relationship with me. As I finally learned to cope with these sad experiences in my life, I realized that I was strong enough to make it through anything with my Savior's help.

One of the hardest new ideas to accept, but which proved to be the most effective in my healing, was that I was not defined by my past successes or failures. Dr. Morrison and Cheri were extremely patient when in many desperate moments over the five years I argued with them that I was not worth saving, a false belief system stemming from residual of abuse.

They pointed me to Christ for my ultimate healing, and with their help, I came to know that my Father in Heaven and Savior *really* love me. Their love is gentle and perfect and encompasses even the hard-to-love parts of us, which, when given soft attention, can become our strengths. With my Savior's help, I came to realize and accept that I was not born into a Garden of Eden, but a Garden of Trials. I was barely beginning to learn that my trials could make me *stronger* as I learned not to blame others for them, but used them as teaching tools to climb back up the ladder to my Heavenly Father. I realized that my greatness would be determined by how well I endured the trials customized for my edification and growth. I felt that now was the time for me to stop being a victim and look forward to a victorious recovery.

The further links I forged down in Provo reconnected me to my true self. I found it so ironic that all these years we had gone to such extremes to match my desperate situation, but what was getting real results was a combination of facing the past and seeing in a new light. I was feeling stronger than ever—a new version of an athlete ready to take on the very opponent who had taken my voice in the beginning.

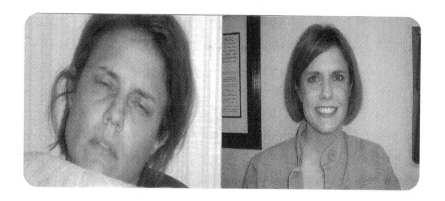

Before and after
Age 35, just six months meeting
with Dr. Morrison (both pictures
taken in her clinic)

Link 21:

Hope through the Process of Forgiveness

"I, the Lord, will forgive whom I will forgive,
but of you it is required to forgive all men."
~Doctrine and Covenants 64:10

Even though I had found much healing in the arms of great physicians, I needed to apply it to the real world. It was March 21, 2011. It had been 14 years since I had run into a friend at a wedding reception in Salt Lake, where I was given a personal challenge to confront my abuser. As she and I got talking and started matching up names of people we both knew, a name in common unfortunately came up. Yes, she too had almost the exact same story to tell regarding childhood abuse by the same corrupt pediatrician. All of a sudden I wasn't alone anymore. As our conversation climaxed and we drew closer, she taught me how she found healing by writing a letter to Dr. Strover, which she later delivered to bring her some closure.

I cringed, thinking how I could never imagine doing this myself. I shivered at the thought of him reading about my feelings and *remembering* me. Sick to my stomach, I couldn't stand him even reminiscing about what he did to me. Putting it into printed words would be accepting it as reality, and a weird thought came to me that if I could forget it as best as I could, it would somehow go away—especially far from him.

But as I recalled, 14 years later, this intimate heart-to-heart with my courageous friend, I knew it was time to let myself find a new level of healing. After having felt the love and mercy of Jesus Christ in my own life, I knew that He would require of me to forgive all men, even as He did, and leave all judgment to His infinite justice. I couldn't go back and wipe out the fact that the abuse happened, but I could, with real intent, follow in the footsteps of my Savior and try with all my heart to begin to forgive the man who hurt me, if only to get on with the rest of my life. The first step would be to scribe my desire to forgive him. I hoped one day to face him in person, but this seemed too daunting at the time, so a letter came first.

I stumbled over the words, starting the letter and then stopping, only to pick it up again several months later. Eventually, though, with the Lord's strength, I was able to write the things of my soul.

Dr. Strover,

I ran into your son the other evening at a viewing, and because it bothered me so much, I knew that I needed to write this letter to you in order for me to release this heavy burden.

Between the ages of five and ten, I had something extremely precious stolen away from me by you. It was my innocence. For 33 years, I have longed to see you in the obituaries in the hope that when you left this mortal life so would the haunting memory of your abuse to me as a child.

I realized, though, in the last few weeks that God held my ticket to peace, not your existence. I see now that we all make mistakes, and that even someone like you (maybe even more so) needs a note like this from someone you hurt long ago.

What happened when I was a child was so very wrong, and I have lived with resentment and anguish because of your actions. I am writing this letter now because I realize that somehow our Savior has already paid the price for your actions and my pain.

I am not completely innocent. I have held a bitter cup to your name, your family, and my parents for the choices you made as a pediatrician. I too am at fault. I realize now that taking you to court or relying on your death to bring me peace was a sin in itself. I have no clue if you have gone through the repentance process and this is not for me to judge. I am only responsible for releasing you from the shackles of my memory and letting the poison out that has haunted me for more than 33 years.

I give my pain and sorrow and imprisonment over to my Savior, for I know I am far from perfect and have an eternity to work on my weaknesses.

Am I hurt that my life is not what I imagined and free from yucky memories? Yes!! But, my stronger regret would be to hold onto the pain our Savior is so willing and eager to take from me. I do not want His sacrifice to go in vain.

I release you from my hatred and anger. I forgive you for your bad choices.

I release you from my nightmares and hateful undertones of all that has plagued me in the hidden corners of my life.

I pray that if there are others wondering what they lost which disabled them from functioning in this world, that they may realize—as I have—what might have happened to them in your exam room long ago and know that the atonement can help free them like it has me in the last four years.

On some level, I think someone out there may have taken away your innocence at some time in your life. It is possible that I, and many others, may have been a product of your past abuse.

I am not your Savior and I don't claim this letter to have any merit except that I want to be free from the chains that bind my soul for hating you all these years. One day I hope to live the words I am writing and truly rid myself of all the unkind feelings I have towards you and your family. My prayer is also that you can forgive me for those feelings.

I am writing this to begin the process of sincerely declaring it to be as if the abuse never happened and to move forward. I have many hard, long days ahead of me and pray that this is the first step to lasting healing in both of us.

I vow to work on it till it's gone—even if it takes until the day I see our Savior face to face.

I know there is goodness in you because you are a son of a loving Heavenly Father and also because your wife must have seen your goodness to stay by your side. I have repeatedly heard what an amazing woman she is, and I must agree.

I have had it witnessed to me that [Christ] loves you just as much as me and possibly even more.

You are a spirit with feelings, emotions, and—most importantly—a heart that can break just like mine did many years ago because of your actions. My heart is even more broken now because I did not allow the Savior to take this from me earlier in life.

Lastly, I forgive you. I forgive you. I forgive you in the only name possible to help me do so, my Beloved Savior and Redeemer, Jesus Christ.

Sincerely,
Peggy

After finishing the letter, I felt like I was in shock. I was not prepared for the heartache that came when I taped the letter to Dr. Strover's front door—too afraid to ring the doorbell and wait, for fear he might answer. I hurried to my parked car on the curb when his sweet wife opened the door and removed the envelope, staring up at me in wonderment. I felt her heart fall as we experienced a meaningful eye exchange, and I softly said, "That is for your husband." It dawned on me that I wasn't the first (or likely the last) person who had left a letter like mine. Slowly, my resentment was evolving into sorrow for what this woman must have felt all these years. Somehow my forgiveness for her husband's crime was replaced with empathy for his family—which my parents had tried to express to me years prior, though the thickness of my pain blocked me from seeing anyone else's pain. His family's heartache hit me full on, making me feel vulnerable. A thought came to me that, truthfully, *this was not all about me.*

I had not been home longer than five minutes after delivering the letter when Brother Young and Brother Thomas from my current ward's Bishopric were standing at my door ringing the bell. I invited them in to sit and visit with my family. These men knew nothing of my errand, but here they were asking my family and me to speak in sacrament meeting on Sunday in a few weeks on the glorious subject of hope. I couldn't believe my ears.

As I listened to them I was thinking they could not possibly have known my struggles, but my Heavenly Father knew. Tears came to my eyes as I came to understand that the timeline of my life didn't matter to God as much as the moments when I began to surrender my pain to Him. I needed to reach out and attempt to forgive the man who had offended me for many years, causing me to suffer.

As these two wonderful brethren continued to visit with my husband and our children, I again recounted in my mind how I had slowly walked up to Dr. Strover's house, mustering as much courage as I could, and yet only had the strength to tape my letter to the front door. Did the pain all go away with the letter? Not completely. I knew it would still take hours on my knees in prayer, pleading for a gradual recovery to let go of the pain. The process of healing would continue. In the meantime, my family and I had been given an assignment to hope.

This was the beginning of me sharing my story. As I risked opening up my heart to others out there suffering, I could feel a new connection to my inner worth. I had years and layers still to uncover with the Spirit cementing the truth into my fragile, uncertain heart.

I knew there was one last, dark link I needed to face in order to finally feel free of my perpetrator. Yet, I wasn't sure if I could ever muster up enough courage to make it happen.

Link 22:

Facing "The One"

"My whole frame doth tremble exceedingly while attempting to speak unto you, but the Lord supports me."
~Mosiah 2:30

Not long after my family's speaking assignment on hope, I felt an itch. I had had five long years of intense therapy with Dr. Morrison and Cheri, and now I desired to go after my dream of becoming a motivational speaker.

I took a Professional Public Speaking course from the talented Kathy Loveless of Loveless Enterprises up in the Avenues. One of my assignments was to first consider who my audience would be, as this would form a good portion of our content and purpose as a speaker. I knew the best place to begin was on my knees. While praying, I got the distinct feeling that I needed to face "the one" before I could ever face anyone else experiencing abuse. I felt I might be facing a group of sexually abused women one day, and I wondered how I could possibly ask them to do something I had not done myself: finding peace and forgiveness from the source of my pain.

I had not yet confronted my own abuser face to face. He was a man I avoided daily for 34 years in my neighborhood, at grocery stores, funerals, and even hospitals (after hearing he had become a phlebotomist years back after his pediatrician license was revoked). Even though I had delivered the letter within the last year, I had to do some searching to find his unlisted phone number. I suddenly felt a fleet of supporters—maybe angels—giving me extra guidance and protection and letting me know I would not be alone in this journey. This is similar to what I felt the summer before as I delivered the letter to his home.

I finally found the phone number and invited him and his wife to join my family at my parents' home the following Sunday evening to find some permanent closure. I had only three days to prepare, and a feeling of shock came over me as the hours closed in on me that Sunday. I wondered what in the world I had done. I felt like a tough dog barking at every passerby only because he is behind a safe barrier, but now the gate had been left ajar with nothing between me and my will to face the object of all my nightmares. I wanted to run and hide. Yes, I had declared it in type, but face-to-face was a whole new ball game. It was the State Championship of my life!

An hour before the meeting I was at church, reverently listening to my friend Linda Harvey's Relief Society lesson, trying to take my mind off of what was about to transpire. Right then, I felt like getting up and running—but from what? Linda's lesson was beautiful, inspiring, but I needed the feel of pavement under my feet, transporting me back to my teenage years when running was more than a physical escape, but a mental one also. Flashes of his stale and shadowy exam room appeared as vivid as if no time had passed. I could see the textured fabric of the curtains, the patterns in the tile. What had I done? Why had I put this in motion to relive this nightmare? It contradicted my every instinct.

The hour passed. I sat in my parents' serene living room waiting for him to show up. I turned to Pam, my dear sister-in-law who believed my childhood confession, and said, "Here we go, down into the deep ocean to face the shark."

"No, Peggy," she said, squeezing my hand. "This time you are rising above the water."

The moment was like a merging of two lost females who had never met before, greeting in a prison cell with the key: me as an abused, fearful little girl and my current 39-year-old self who had been hit by the resulting emotional shrapnel. The two prisoners met and merged into *one* as I was finally facing the man who selfishly took away my innocence. The words I had rehearsed in Dr. Morrison's office so many times in an attempt to find freedom was now a living reality, no longer just a pep talk in my head.

I had gone into this not really expecting anything from him. This was MY time to face him, to reclaim my voice and move forward—never again shrinking into myself if I happened to see him in public. I wanted my freedom back! Dr. Strover's wife had told me that her husband was still living in delusion and that he denied the things that went on in his medical practice. She warned me that this was an illness, so I prepared myself to give my declaration as a recovering victim and attempt to bring closure. Yes, I had sent him the letter, but that had been a practice run. This was the real deal.

This was the scene on that Sunday evening. Along with Pam, my husband and parents were there with me, waiting for the doctor and his wife in their beautiful living room, a place where I found much safety and peace, as it carried a sweet spirit of happy memories from countless family celebrations over the years.

I was shocked at how automatic it was for me to cover my chest with a pillow, as if needing to hide *anything* about me that might attract him. It became clear to me why many who are abused might, as a defense mechanism, go to extremes to be less attractive to the opposite sex. I firmly moved the pillow away from me and tried to sit up tall, to reclaim my ground as a safe, strong female.

Dr. Strover, who was in his mid-eighties, and his wife arrived right on time and took their seats across the room from Steve and me. The time was now. Here was the man whose selfish actions had been the source of so much pain in my life. This was the moment I never dreamed would happen—the moment I never wanted to take place, yet I if I wanted to truly move forward, it had to.

I took a deep breath and asked him straight out, "Do you know why you're here, Graham?" (I called him by his first name; I did not have the respect to call him doctor.)

He said, "Yes. It's because you wrote me a beautiful letter last summer." Perplexed but determined, I asked him again if he knew why he was there and, just as his wife had warned me, he replied, "No, I looked through my charts, but couldn't find yours," as if he would have carelessly charted sexual abuse in his notes. This was no shocker. My mom had warned me that he would deny it, as she had heard him deny other things during earlier acquaintances, but she told me to get my feelings out no matter what.

Disgusted that he still had files of his past patients, I cringed and responded, "What you did was very wrong. You molested me."

He then said how sorry he was for hurting me, even though he could not remember what had happened. His words sounded rehearsed and empty, as if a lawyer had role-played with him to keep him safe without disclosing any convicting details.

I proceeded to let him know how this meeting was going to play out. Steve would offer a prayer because we definitely needed God as the director of this scene, then I would read another letter (which contained more detail of the pain I experienced because of abuse), Pam would share some thoughts, and then my mother would comment. I was controlling, to say the least, but I had been the victim of this mental, toxic power struggle far too long and I was through letting Dr. Strover's manipulation trump my voice. He was in *my* office now.

In the letter I read aloud, I explained that I, too, would need to face my Maker, watch my life in review, and acknowledge the many mistakes I made in this mortal life, and that not *all* that had happened was his fault. I assured him that I had considered taking him to court, but each time I prayed over the decision I was comforted by our Heavenly Father that the court He would hold with him in heaven would be more powerful and permanent than any court I could put him through on this earth. I went on to say that I had already wasted so many of my years and it was time for me to move forward and trust that God would handle justice. My part in this was to find forgiveness along with finding my voice.

Pam told stories of three other women who had young daughters around my same age who were also affected by Dr. Strover's sexual abuse. For several years she had worked with a mental health group for families struggling with mental illness who had openly confessed in three separate sessions during Addiction Week that their daughters all had issues stemming from the same man, their pediatrician. Sheepishly, Dr. Strover responded that he had no idea he had caused so much pain. As most perpetrators do, he tried to flip the table by presenting a sorry case, saying I had no clue what he had been through when he lost the medical practice he had spent years building. It was as if he was the victim, not the patients he violated.

In the same moment my sweet mother spoke up. No one had given her a voice yet. It shocked all of us, as she is usually so non-confrontational. Calling him by name, she said, "You tricked me. What you told me was medically necessary was a lie. Peggy did not cry in your office, but she did in the days before and the days to follow. You sexually molested her!" Nothing ever said that day would ever be as powerful as that statement. Her voice and body shook as she stood up to him, and in that moment all my faith in her was beginning to be restored as if the years of devastation had never happened between us.

"You were never in the room," spat Dr. Strover.

Red-faced, my mother stated she would never have left her child alone in a doctor's room. With conviction purer than crisp, cold air, she declared, "You did it right in front of me. Don't deny it!"

As Mom spoke, Dr. Strover's memory seemed to quickly lift and his next reply completely contradicted his previous statement of not having any recollection of my files or history. "I had to check Peggy. She had a medical condition and this is what I was taught to do in my medical training." As if it were as simple as pulling a rotten tooth, he discarded each accusation with a classic answer, deflecting the real issue. My blood was boiling. He had a comeback for every accusation and an alibi that was just as coy.

Not only was his physical touch a poison, but his mental twisting and manipulation was so brilliant it was no wonder he had gotten away with it for as long as he did. All of the teachers and mentors I had resisted because of the controlling way they talked to me were spotlighted in that moment, all because of Dr. Strover's masterminded deceit. All along he had been the trigger for my resistance, not the innocent people I had deflected my anger on throughout the years.

In that powerful moment I realized that my tender mother had been just as abused as I had been by this sick man, yet she had suffered in different ways. He had gained and betrayed her trust years before his medical practice as a high school friend. I understood now that my mother had been carrying her guilt for far too long, and I needed to reassure her that she too was free, even if it took years for my heart to soften and the coarse shell of pride I had built up against her to break. Regardless of the reality of feeling like I was not heard as a child, Mom and Dad truly had not realized the extent of the damage done in his office.

Even though I felt the mental anguish caused by his deceit and manipulation starting some 34 years prior, I said to him, "The abuse is over. It is over!"

I thought that as soon as I made my declaration the pain of the past would be swallowed up as quickly as it had entered my life. I was surprisingly off. Peace was furthest from my emotions. Anger had replaced it, kindling a wild fire so powerful I felt like exploding all over everyone.

Dr. Strover asked me what he could do, so I told him to write a letter to anyone and everyone whom he may have affected with his abuse. He and his wife explained how costly that would be. This pushed me over the edge. I expressed that I didn't think he picked favorites and that there might be hundreds out there who also needed closure from his dirty addiction. He could never be able to comprehend the damage he had done to so many.

"There is no price you could put on the damage your actions have caused, do you comprehend this?" I said. Silence fell. I realized I was getting nowhere. It was time to leave, what was said was said, and the little girl in me was finally ready to walk out of his office once and for all.

I hurried past Dr. Strover, telling him I was through, and ran into the TV room where I cried out the leftover shock at how manipulative and delusional he still was—even when we gave him the chance to confess all and make amends. To his credit, he did apologize to my parents after I stormed out, saying he was sorry for the pain he had caused and would keep a safe distance from our family.

Pam followed me to provide comfort, and I cried like I never have before, as if the floodgates of hell had been released and all its toxins were flushed away. This had been the real deal! The shock was equal to the power it took to face him and own my voice once and for all.

When Steve and my parents came in, my mom said to me, "Peggy, where did you come from?" I asked her what she meant. She continued, "I couldn't believe your courage." I realized then just how scared my mom had been all these years. She had taught me poise and elegance, but I was the last link in our family to come along to teach her courage in the face of hard truths she tried to avoid because of guilt, feeling responsible for all these years. This was one of the most extraordinary mother-daughter healing moments I could ever imagine as we faced *the one* together.

Link 23:

Releasing the Pain to the Savior

"Come unto me, all ye that labour and are heavy laden,
and I will give you rest. Take my yoke upon you, learn of me;
for I am meek and lowly in heart: and ye shall find rest unto
your souls. For my yoke is easy, and my burden is light."
~Matthew 11:28-30

The next morning I awoke with the most dark, heavy feeling of disappointment and confusion. Facing the doctor had been the key, I thought, to getting my voice back. I had declared my abuse, as I had rehearsed, and stated emphatically that it would *never* happen again. This is what the little girl inside me needed to have happen, and yet the residue of mental torment lingered like the soapy film on dishes having gone through a wash cycle but not coming out crystal clean.

So what was off? I had given myself the eight seconds of courage to make the call and my moment of truth to meet with the doctor and his wife, but the weight of the abuse still stuck like a fly with one wing caught in a web. It was true that the spider had been sprayed with a pesticide, but something else was keeping me captive in his sticky web. Could it be *me*?

My past coping mechanism kicked in and I went to the gym to try to exercise my unrest away. When it wasn't proving effective, I called my friend Cheri Harris to help me process my thoughts. I described to her the vision of me feeling like a trapped fly in a spider's web. My spider (abuser) had been sprayed with pesticide, unable to hurt me any longer, yet I still had one un-freed wing. Cheri asked me what it would take to unstick it and fly away.

162

Troubled by the question, I closed my eyes and went to my "inner knowing" connecting me to God. Listening intently to what He was trying to teach me, I pictured my Savior reaching to pull me out of that nasty web—a web I had, paradoxically, become comfortable with for almost four decades. My Savior was reaching with the intent to take something from me so that I might be loosed from the bands of torment, but what was it? I had faced the man who haunted my childhood dreams, and I thought I had forgiven him.

In that moment I felt a sliver in my side being removed, a sliver of *hatred* being pulled out by the Redeemer. Would I let it go? It had been a part of me for so long now. Who would I blame for my resentment, pain, and anguish if I let go of that sliver? As the Savior pulled, I felt like I was pulling back, claiming this wound as a part of me, as if my identity had become the mask of a victim. At this point I knew what was keeping me from flying away from the web of abuse, this home of deception in which I had become comfortable. It had worked for me for so long I was hesitant to release myself and feel what it truly meant to be free of the label—"victim"—that had defined me for so long. It was not the doctor of my past holding me hostage. It was my *anger* and *hate,* an addiction more potent than the abuse itself.

"Forgive the mortal man you called doctor," was the plea my Savior was making to me. "That's all it will take to be free." Though I thought I had forgiven him many times over, I knew this time would have to be different. I didn't know who I would be once I had truly broken free from resentment, anger, and guilt. It had become my barricade, halting the process of healing.

It took everything I had to unstick my trapped wing and offer the Savior my pain and prison that had become my background noise for so many years. Pulling and tugging, I loosened my wing and faced the spider—my perpetrator—and left his web for good. The Savior offered me His hand and I took it.

The beauty of my journey is not that I was able to face the man who took what was not his to take, but that my loving Redeemer Jesus Christ was *always* there to be my strength, especially when I felt most alone. I just had to trust Him and be willing to let go. The mental trap was real, but the illusion was that I needed my perpetrator's permission to fly away. In my struggle, I myself had weaved a web more intricate and sticky than any the perpetrator could have woven. Yes, it was horrific to have been abused for five consecutive years, but the Savior through His atonement offered me a way out of the pain if I would but reach for Him to set me free.

Forgiveness is a process. Each day I have to remind myself how easy it is to get trapped in the web so long as I hold myself in the past. Though my past was painful, there is a balm to free me each time I fall for the adversary's lie that I am not free to choose forgiveness and happiness. I *am* free! I am no longer a victim chained to my abuse. I get to choose each day as I wake if I will stay stuck in Satan's deceitful web of lies where I cannot fly, or loosen my wings and believe in the redeeming power of the Atonement.

It is my choice to be free, regardless of how many times I need to be reminded of it from here on out. As long as I give God the keys to my heart and turn over my will, there will never be chains strong enough that cannot be broken!

The question now isn't so much if I can break the chains, but what will I do with the links of lessons I have experienced?

The Innocent Link:

Q&A between mother and daughter

"Her children arise up, and call her blessed."

~Proverbs 31:28

I begin to close where I began. Nineteen years after Steve and I married, we made a drastic move this past year to sell both our home and my parents' home (Steve and I at age 41 and my parents at 84) and move in together, combining not only our living space but our traditions—from supper to laundry times. For my parents, leaving their home after 43 years was beyond heart wrenching. Memories cried out from the plaster walls as we lowered the last painting. Children's measurements marked behind the door of the medicine cabinet captured childhood merging into adulthood. With humble hearts, friends and family gathered one last time, remembering Sunday dinners around the *Warner Hearth*. Grandchildren climbed and swung on the rope swing hanging from the sycamore in the front yard. Grandma and Grandpa Warner knew memories like these are made but once in a lifetime.

Mom had to be compelled away from the house in the final hours as she reminisced over the generations that had run through those hallways, climbed the laundry chute, and danced under the flocked Christmas tree while she played her famous tune on the baby grand piano tucked in the bay window. Her heart tore as she relinquished the keys to a new matriarch, yet she was willing to see how Dad and she needed extra attention in their golden years.

Dad, just as sentimental but more practical, adjusted more seamlessly than Mom. Five months later, just shy of Mom's 85th birthday, she had a terrible fall, breaking five ribs and puncturing a lung, landing her in respite care for over a month. Not long after, Dad took an unexpected fall of his own, though not a physical one. He had been taking it easy after a massive heart attack ten months prior, but this was a different decline. He and I spent hours tending to bills and visiting Mom. His stalwart confidence of "You Gotta Believe" was steadily dissipating, echoing Mom's dire circumstances, as if he were being summoned heavenward when no one was watching.

Dad himself may not have completely understood the sun that was setting fast for him, but his life hinted towards a mission yet to serve. Special visitors blessed our abode, as if preparing the way for him to go home. Sacred conversations were had with his own mother, brother, and even his best friend gracing the walls of the new home he had nested my mom safely in before flying into his son Dave's open arms.

In his final days, Dad, resistant, looked at me and thanked me for being his daughter, as he did with each of his children. He didn't play favorites except when it came to his beloved wife. She came first for over 63 years, since that special day at East High School when he knew the two would be one forever more. As the hours closed in Dad pulled Steve and me close to his bedside and asked us to watch over his precious ruby he called "Neddy." They had always talked of leaving this life together, peacefully in their sleep, but this wasn't the ending God had in mind. Dad left us early in the morning on September 12, 2013, next to his loving wife.

To be honest, I have wondered since why God didn't grant them this wish. What on earth would this saintly woman have left to finish as a mortal before graduating into Christ's arms? Then the prompting I have felt before quiets my heart as I contemplate, like usual, Mom stayed at the party a little longer to make sure everything was right in the lives of the people she cared about.

Mom and I never really asked the hard, painful questions surrounding the abuse, as it was such a thorn of guilt in her side. Being under the same roof, frozen emotions have begun to thaw. Pressure emerged out of stress and desperation for a man who seemed to know how to ease our differences. Dad was the peacemaker when shadows of the past rose up.

"Respect your mother," his devoted tongue would scold me if the little girl inside reached for the bitterness of the past. "She doesn't deserve your unkind words." He knew Mom was innocent of my pain, yet my pride to fully let go of what was out of her control was holding her captive for years now. Even though I had told her several times that if I believed I agreed to this trial, then of course I would have been given a mother who couldn't recognize the abuse happening, in order for it to take place. I meant it, yet the words fell empty as the pressure between us raged on. As triggers of control tightened around me, I became like the little girl from my past, needing to fully address buried emotions between us.

When I began writing this book, I thought its purpose would be to provide a theory or platform on how I believed I agreed to my trials, but the Lord has allowed my heart to wrestle until a truer purpose of this process arose out of desperation to understand how to connect my links. Then one night this past February after watching a wonderful rendition of Les Misérables at Hale Center Theater with Steve, it hit me.

This journey of facing these haunting memories and capturing them in script has been for various reasons, but most importantly it was to loosen the shackles I had placed on my mom. She is the innocent link. For almost 42 years she has been the hero in my life. She bore the tantrums and loved me despite them. She took the rebellious teen head on and loved me anyway. She observed the over-spending adult and chose to see only the good in my well-intentioned heart.

God is brilliant. I believe He knew what would motivate me to begin writing my story, even if at times it was solely for me, as I would pour out my heart (which could feel like passing an emotional kidney stone) while experiencing anger, resentment, forgiveness, acceptance, and remorse during the process. Most of the time the darkness would pass and the magic of releasing my pain through the text would boomerang back to me. As I ended each entry with my conviction that I truly agreed to my trials, I could see their benefits. Gratefully, each time my team of many helpers had me revise, I would find my words turning softer and gentler for all those involved. Each version seemed to either dig deeper into areas I didn't want to face or heal those areas that showed continued hostility.

I am mortal, but my goal is to one day have no trace of leftover residue of the power struggle Mom and I still seem to face today. This is my present link. It is as if God knew my mom and I needed to come full circle and face those hard moments we had not truly confronted, before she graduates from this earthly classroom. It is as if we have been locked in a closet with the intent of facing what we had both run from in different ways for 40-plus years. I realize just how truly gracious a woman she has been for putting up with me as I've recovered from the mounds of emotional rubble. She gets the prize no earthly possession could reward!

If there is a common thread to be found among people who have experienced trauma, it is that there is usually one person scapegoated to take the spotlight off the abuse itself. My mom has been the person I have hurt the most. I know that, although she didn't know the abuse was happening, she (like Christ) accepted the role as the one who would bear my heartache. Was this fair? No! Was she deserving of it? In no way possible.

If I were to leave you with an invitation it would be to let go of the chains we hold around not only ourselves but around those who may have accepted the role of being your soft place to land. Mother, brother, sister, husband, friend, or father—these people hold many names, but the common denominator they all share is that they deserve the gold medal for putting up with the grit of what we haven't understood about ourselves. It is time to link ourselves to the beautiful parts of empathy, as no one is spared from heartache down here.

The following questions should have been asked years ago. Writing this book has had a more prophetic impact on me than anyone else, as I have been able to lay out on the table my past and examine it, seeing how it was all meant for my good. Healing the wound but leaving the scar, as a blessing that comes with heartache, has taught invaluable lessons. As I asked my mom these hard questions, tears and heartache fell between us as the healing powers of heaven illuminated that her silence for all these years was not out of not caring, merely out of not knowing what to say.

I invite you, if you can relate, to please ask the hard questions. They truly mend hearts. Pain only has power when the past stays secret and hidden. To soothe this pain, the past must be resolved and relationships mended between all involved. Please don't waste another minute. Reach out, start to mend, open a closet which seems too dreadful to face. Will it be worth it? Beyond any prize imaginable, because as you do hearts will open, heal, and the truth will set free what was always meant to be.

You are worth it! Those you love are worth it! As we extend forgiveness where it is least expected, the Lord blesses us beyond all fears holding the process back. I promise you with all my heart that forgiveness is possible! Take the first step; use those eight seconds of courage you have stored away just waiting to be tapped into. It's your turn!

CB

PEGGY: What were your initial thoughts and feelings when Pam and I asked you not to take me back to the pediatrician?

NEDRA: None of my children had liked to go to the doctor, so I figured your behavior was normal.

PEGGY: When you found out he had been caught doing inappropriate things, what did you feel?

NEDRA: I felt terrible! We stopped going to him, but I still didn't know what else was going on relating to Peggy or anyone else.

PEGGY: Did you ever doubt Dr. Strover's "diagnoses" or methods? Were you afraid to doubt him?

NEDRA: No, I didn't doubt him because he talked to me like a doctor talked to a mother. His medical explanation sounded logical how he phrased it. His deceit was very well hidden by logic. Peggy, you never cried while he was doing it. If you would have screamed I wouldn't have taken you back. He was wise and smart and knew how to phrase his lies. It was only a five minute visit, so it didn't seem like you were being hurt.

PEGGY: Did you ever, even once, attribute my behavior (tantrums, teenage angst, etc.) to the abuse?

NEDRA: No, I didn't. I didn't know why you were having tantrums. I didn't know why you were acting out as a teen. I knew I loved you, and whatever you were going through I would help you through it.

PEGGY: When you were with me to confront the doctor, how were you feeling? What were you thinking? What did you hope would be revealed or come out of this meeting?

170

NEDRA: I had told you the day before we met with him that he would deny it, and to ask him straight out about it. I knew because he had denied other things he would do the same with this. He made me feel extremely angry. Horribly. The thought that he was there and [Gill and I] couldn't do anything about it was horrible. We hadn't the courage to let him in the house; Peggy, you had the courage. We had been concerned about hurting his wife and plainly did not know what to do. I was shaking and crying on the couch when he was there because of what he had done to you. I was hoping he would confess but he did not. He denied it all. He said sorry, but denied it all. It made me furious. The only good thing was that he finally knew now how we all felt.

PEGGY: If you were given the opportunity to talk to a mother experiencing the same difficulty with her child, what would you say to her? What advice and hope would you give?

NEDRA: Just listen to her and find out really what she is saying, and believe her.

PEGGY: What is the most important thing you want me—and all girls who have experienced abuse—to know?

NEDRA: That there is a place to heal and everyone is different in the way they heal. Even though your guardians may not know how to connect with you, or it's too hard to process with you, we still hurt when you hurt, regardless of our ability to communicate this. As mothers, it's a lifelong burden to see our daughters suffer throughout the years. I wish it had never happened, but if it has I pray for some way you can find healing too. Please forgive your mothers.

PEGGY: What can you say to parents out there who have not yet addressed this with their children who have walked a similar path?

NEDRA: Please listen to them and see where they can be helped. These predators who do this to our children should be accused and put in jail. I wish I would have pressed charges. He is still out there not under the sex offenders list. The time has passed for our family to take him to court, as he is in his eighties, but we have left the judgment of God for him to be tried in Heaven. Seek help. Don't wait. You deserve to be heard.

PEGGY: Do you feel he abused you as well as abusing me?

NEDRA: Of course, twice as much. He gained my trust by grooming me as friends then lied to me to get to my child. To the mothers out there wondering if they ought to trust their feelings and tell someone, PLEASE TELL. You're worth it and so is your child! It is not your fault for not knowing, but it's what you do with the knowledge that matters.

PEGGY: Will you forgive me for placing so much blame and anger towards you?

NEDRA: Of course I will, honey, of course. I always have.

To the mothers and other guardians out there who didn't know: Truth is we are all doing the best with what we are given in spite of the past. It is time to forgive each other and move forward. We love you dearly!

Forever bonded in love

Link 25:

Vantage Points

"A friend loves at all times,
and a brother is born for adversity."
~Proverbs 17:17

I love people! I truly feel God sent angels down to help me through dark times when I was a young girl and on into my adulthood. I wanted in some way to include those who have sweat long, long hours with me. I believe it is so helpful to have many perspectives and vantage points of abuse, so I asked those closest to my past to share their wise insight. I am very aware that not everyone has a support system like I have had; therefore, I am humbled and feel blessed to share these precious outlooks with you as additional eyes, in the hopes that somehow they will inspire those of us who are bystanders to someone being abused. When I read, especially, Alecia's portion I was in tears, as she could have put in countless wrongs I had done in high school to hurt our precious friendship and it would have all been true. I was careless and choose a poor choice above our lifelong friendship. A regret I will take to my grave, yet as you will read she only remembered the tender moments between us, showing me again just how blessed I truly am to have persons like Alecia and the following in my life. I don't deserve any of them, but I will treasure them nonetheless.

CR

Alecia Thompson Williams on childhood memories

It would be impossible to reflect on my childhood without happy memories of Peggy Warner. She was a huge part of my life. I have countless memories of two young girls who were always up for an adventure and who—without fail—loved to laugh.

Peggy and I had the uncanny ability to laugh uncontrollably at just about anything, and we were also quite good at laughing at all the wrong times (which often got us into trouble).

Even a mundane task of driving around running errands with our moms was filled with laughter. I have distinct memories of the two of us sitting in the back seat of her mom's white Crown Victoria, barely containing ourselves as we challenged each other to see who could do the deepest, longest laugh before running out of breath.

We both attended a private elementary school—a school that focused on order and manners. The administration quickly learned that it was in the teacher's best interest to keep us as far apart as possible. When class got long and slow, which I recall happening several times a day, Peggy and I would cope by trying to get the other person to laugh—even from our desks on opposite sides of the room. All we needed to do was pull what we referred to as "The Mr. Furley"—a facial expression based on the Don Knotts character from the popular sitcom "Three's Company." When Mr. Furley got angry, he would hold his head really still, but with a subtle shake. His eyes would bulge out and with tightly pursed lips, he would slowly turn his face towards the person who had wronged him. We thought it was hilarious and learned to mimic him perfectly.

We loved this face and found it was the ideal way to communicate with each other in class because it didn't even require eye contact. Sometimes, all I needed was to see Peggy's hair begin to shake and I knew that "Mr. Furley" was coming. Neither of us could contain ourselves, and I am sure that it always surprised the teacher when the two of us could blurt out laughing at exactly the same time on opposite sides of the room.

Those days usually ended with a trip to Mr. John's office, our principal, where we were once again challenged to hold our laughter as we tried to apologize for such inappropriate behavior.

We thought we were hilarious, but as I sit back and think about those countless trips to the principal's office, we were pretty funny— or, at the very least, we had fun.

Peggy and I were such good friends. Our summers were filled with long bike rides to the Tennis Club, sleepovers on her trampoline, swimming and long talks about boys, and plans for our future and how we were always going to be best friends, live right next door to each other and watch our kids become best friends too.

When I was 11 years old, my family moved from my childhood home. I will be honest when I admit that I was scared and insecure wondering how I would survive without the friendship of my dear friend Peggy. Fortunately, both of our parents recognized our special joined-at-the-hip friendship and provided countless opportunities for us to spend our weekends together.

Oftentimes my dad would pick her up on his way home from work and then Peggy would stay with us until her parents came to get her on Sunday. Those were happy weekends. We usually took the $20 bill that her parents provided for "necessities," and we would head straight to the candy aisle at Albertson's grocery store.

For the rest of the weekend, we would do what we always did best—perfect the skill of laughing until it hurt.

One particular weekend, when I was around 13 years old, my parents were out of town and had hired a young lady to babysit my five siblings and me. For some reason, this babysitter felt compelled during her short stay to discipline us in a way that was completely opposite from my parents' approach and the more we resisted, the more determined she became to "change our ways."

By the time Peggy arrived on Friday, the tug-of-war with the babysitter was in full swing. Fortunately, my siblings and I had identified all the right buttons to push to send the babysitter over the edge and the fact that she hated laughter was a recipe for disaster.

As soon as Peggy walked in the door, the two of us felt like we were still sitting in our 6th grade class, pulling "Mr. Furley" faces and laughing uncontrollably. By Sunday morning, the babysitter was at her wits end. As she desperately tried to gather us for early morning church, we decided to get dressed up in the most ridiculous old lady outfits we could configure.

We scrounged through my mom's closet and found a few ill-fitting dresses, old jewelry, and some shawls. We draped ourselves in the clothes and tried to make ourselves look as ridiculous and pathetic as possible. To this day, I still laugh out loud as I picture the three of us walking down the stairs with straight faces and climbing into the babysitter's car acting like heavily sedated old ladies. Peggy stayed "in character" during the entire time at church. She had her head wrapped in a peach, silk shawl, and she would stare off with a pitiful empty stare. It was absolutely hilarious—at least to us.

Once we got home, we laughed until we cried. The babysitter went berserk and packed up her things and quit. Even hours after she was gone, we would burst into laughter, celebrating our victory. My sister Marisa and I still reminisce about that weekend and how laughter with Peggy saved us.

It would be impossible to recount the endless stories I have of Peggy, but it goes without saying that they were always full of laughter and fun. I am sure that we drove people crazy. Looking back, even though we had never verbalized it, it was almost as if Peggy and I had made a silent pact to find joy in the mundane and laughter in even the most routine moments of life.

It was a gift and is part of the reason that memories of my childhood are filled with so much happiness and laughter.

Sadly, as we grew in age, life and distance eventually caused our friendship to drift. Our plans to live next to each other have not panned out, but I guess there is still time, right?

After all these years, I still have a deep love for my dear friend Peggy. It has pained me deeply to gradually learn more and more about the horrific abuse that she endured as a child—a side of her life that she somehow shielded from me.

I have often asked myself how someone who was such a central figure in my life for so many years was hurting in a way that I did not fully recognize. Yes, of course, looking back there were signs. More than once, I found her curled up on the floor crying silently in her closet, and it always puzzled me during her teenager years that she was on an endless quest to run away and start her life over somewhere else. During these times, I found that she had a pain that was deeper than anything I had ever known and I did not know how to help my friend.

I could have done more. I should have done more.

As a child, Peggy was silently trying to teach herself to survive and cope from her abuse. She was alone and, looking back, somehow she did it with poise and grace and even more remarkably, she was able to still fill her days with laughter.

I am honored to call her a friend. Her laughter saved me countless times and helped me find joy in life. I guess I can only hope that our laughter saved her a little too.

Ashley Brooks Boyack on friendship

I have known Peggy my whole life. We were friends from as early as you can have a friend. We fought and played as sisters would. I thought at the time that we shared all the secrets that little girls had. We went to a private elementary school together, junior high, and most of high school together.

We went to the same college and even took some of the same college courses. We studied, hung out, and shared every aspect of our lives. My entire adolescent life Peggy tried to save me. She always called me to get me out of the house. She invited me to parties, play dates, "hang outs" at her cabin, a run around the neighborhood, an outing for ice cream, a study session, or just a movie among friends.

She lined me up with countless dates. I dare say I would have never had a first date if it were not for Peggy. If it had not been for her I would have been a lonely little girl. Peggy has always been good at that—finding the lost little sheep and tenderly loving it until it sees it's potential. She did this for me intuitively. She did it out of complete compassion and love. Over the years, I have seen her do this for hundreds. She has the gift to heal the wounded heart. Her ability to show empathy and compassion is above and beyond that of a normal person. It is a gift from God.

As close as we were growing up, I never knew that Peggy harbored a secret that haunted her spirit. Maybe I should have been more cognitive, but it was not until we were both adults that I learned Peggy had absolutely hated to go to her pediatrician when she was a little girl because he examined her in a way that made her want to scream.

People didn't talk about molesting in those days, but pieces of the puzzle started slipping into place. I remember being at her house and talking to her about why she took medication to make her feel better.

We would joke about how it made her lose weight. I had no idea what she was going though at the time.

CR

Pam Warner Childs on abuse

I will never forget the first time I met the 3-year-old pig-tailed Peggy. I couldn't believe how cute she was. You couldn't help but fall in love with that darling little face. As the youngest of seven children, Peggy was very attached to her mom. No one could comfort her but her mother. As time went by, I became an official member of the family and Peggy became a very important person in my life even though she was only 4 years old.

I became pregnant soon after I married Peggy's oldest brother Dave, and Peggy was thrilled. She really wanted a boy because she had a nephew she adored, so she didn't know what it would be like having a girl. She even asked me to take the baby out for a just a few seconds so she could see him.

Of course, I had a girl we named Heidi, and Peggy fell in love with her immediately. Peggy started coming over to our home on a regular basis then to play with Heidi and to help make chocolate chip cookies. Of course, we would eat as much of the dough as the cookies.

When Peggy was five, she started struggling with separation anxiety from people she loved and trusted. She loved spending time with Heidi because for once she was not the youngest. I could see that Peggy struggled with anxiety issues. She cried easily and needed comfort. I knew something was really bothering Peggy, but how does a 5-to-6-year-old express how she feels?

On a particular day it all came to a head. Peggy was at my house and her mother called to let her know that she was picking her up to take her to her doctor's appointment. Peggy became hysterical. She screamed, cried, and ran to my basement and hid behind the washer and dryer. She begged me to keep her safe and not let her mom take her to the doctor. At first I thought she was just afraid of the doctor like most kids, but after a lot of questioning, I realized it was a lot more than just fear of doctors. In her naïve way she explained to me why she was so afraid of this particular doctor. I couldn't believe what I was hearing. I had a daughter of my own I took to a doctor and she was never examined the way Peggy was...Big Red Flag!

What was happening to Peggy was wrong!

I have never witnessed a child so afraid of another human being. When Peggy's mom came to get her I told her how afraid Peggy was and also told her about the way she felt when she was being examined by the doctor. I asked her to please stop taking Peggy to that doctor. Because the doctor had gained such a trust with her mom, and the other children didn't care for the checkups as well, the visits continued.

☙

Amy Nielsen Iverson on the hard years

Peggy and Steve had moved to St. George with their newly adopted little boy. I was without children and living in Texas. I decided to visit them on my way to a girls' getaway in Las Vegas. Although Peggy and I talked often, this was truly the first time I realized Peggy was suffering. She seemed overwhelmed by caring for her toddler and desperate for a friend. She also seemed distant in a way I hadn't seen before. I remember we had planned for me to visit for a few days, and then she would drive me down to meet my friends in Vegas. The day before I was to leave, she asked if I could just drive myself. I was taken aback because there would be a large fee for a rental car. We remedied the situation by asking Steve to come with us so she would not have to drive home alone.

I was concerned, but not sure what to do, yet later learned this was one of the darkest periods of her life. A couple of years later, I had just given birth to twins. Peggy was coming for a visit. At the last minute, she cancelled because she and Steve had word that a birthmother had selected them. Instead, in her usual generous way, she offered her seat on her brother-in-law's private jet to my mother. What a blessing. Soon after, when the would-be adoption fell through, Peggy came. At the time, I'm sure I did not recognize how difficult the trip must have been on her heart. She and Steve were hoping to adopt another child and wanted a baby desperately. I had two. She spent time with me holding the babies without a word of discontent. Within a month, another birthmother chose Peggy and Steve. Grace is just a couple of months younger than those twins, and now she and my daughter, Claire, are dear friends.

Steve and Peggy later flew halfway across the world to visit me when I lived in Bavaria. I was pregnant and my husband was doing military training in another country. We toured all around Germany, sightseeing and taking in the culture. During this time, Peggy was attempting to detox from all her prescription medicines for anxiety and depression. I had not realized she had been taking many, many medications, and it was not easy for her to taper. I recall her shaking and sleeping for hours and hours. How I admired her for pushing forward, amid her struggle.

CR

Julie Debry Labrum on the hard years

While my dear friend Peggy was living in West Jordan, I remember visiting her at her new house for the first time. It had been a while since I had seen her. When she opened the door, I literally did not recognize her. I think it might have been the weight she put on, or the distance in her eyes, but she was not the Peggy I knew. Something had changed and I searched her face for some recognition or resemblance of the fun girl I knew.

I remember it was confusing for me at first, but as I spent time with her, she showed more glimpses of herself. When I met her at the gym close to her house and took her grocery shopping, it was fun to spend time with her. Still, I sensed she was struggling in her surroundings. I wasn't sure what stress she must be under, but she seemed to smile through the times we were together.

I remember when I became more worried about her. One night, Amy and I picked her up for dinner and ice cream, and Peggy was very quiet. She didn't speak much or hold eye contact. Her body language was lethargic. After dinner, we drove to an ice cream shop. Peggy didn't know what she wanted and was unresponsive when I asked her.

We sat at a table to enjoy our dessert when the conversation suddenly ended up between Amy and me. We both looked at Peggy and had an immediate, unspoken concern that was obvious. Peggy's head was on the table, resting barely on her arm, as if asleep, and ice cream was drooling out of the side of her mouth! I wish I had an iPhone back then because that would've been a vivid picture to begin to describe a world where Peggy barely survived—dulled, numb, and even unconsciously going through life.

I tried to understand that the meds Peggy was on at that time desensitized her. It made her feel nothing. She had told me that her doctor regularly tried new combinations and changed meds to keep up with her revolving depression. I now know that the meds were only a Band-Aid for the symptoms surfacing from her abuse.

Many years later, when she began to come off her meds, I remember Peggy describing her senses as being reawakened. She would say that she was sensitive to light and could feel on her fingertips the sense of touch in a new way. And she could smell new things again. Her body had been subdued in a constant fog, and she had to learn how to re-emerge from the dark and begin to live! I am so glad.

◌੭

Pam Warner on confronting the doctor

As I watched Peggy confront her abuser and saw the strength that it took, she was absolutely amazing. She tried to express to him calmly about the part of her life that he took away. She looked at him eye to eye with such courage. I was amazed that she could do such a thing, and it made me grateful that she has made me a small part of her life.

That night was a testimony to me of the Savior's love. Instead of hate in the room, there was just sorrow and pain with everyone trying to forgive and understand that everything that had happened or would happen was now in the Lord's hands.

At one point Peggy needed to finally leave the room. I knew she couldn't be alone so I followed her. We went into the family room. There Peggy broke down and cried harder than I have ever seen her cry. It was as if 30-plus years of torment were being released. My heart broke for her. But I also admired her for what she had just done. What a life journey I have witnessed with Peggy. She is amazing, courageous, beautiful, and a great example to all.

It made me think of all our years together. My [daughter] Heidi really loved Peggy. Sometimes she felt as if the only person who understood her was Peggy. In a lot of ways there were a lot of similarities in Heidi and Peggy. They sounded so much the same that after Heidi died at age 19 and Peggy would call, her voice was a reality check because she sounded so much like Heidi. I think Heidi was a Warner in so many ways and she too, like Peggy, was abused and reacted to the abuse in a similar way. At first she tried to change who she was, trying to become someone else. I only wish Heidi would have

184

lived long enough to learn from Peggy that you can overcome the abuse and learn to love and live again. But as Peggy always reminds me, Dave and Heidi are in a great place where pain, sorrow, and the heartaches of life don't exist. For that I am grateful. Thank you, Peggy, for keeping me grounded when it came to this.

When Peggy was a teenager, she tried so hard to be perfect. She took on tasks like tennis and exercise and went beyond what she should have. You could see that she was trying so hard to work out who she was. She had it in her head that if she looked perfect she would be perfect. She looked great and was in great shape physically, but the struggle continued in her head. She would talk to me about how awful she felt, how she didn't want to eat and how she needed to exercise all the time. I can't speak for Peggy. I can only describe what I observed and understood from her.

I will never forget when she was about ten and sitting around my kitchen table when she delivered the most beautiful news. She said, "I will never have to see my doctor again because his license has been revoked."

It was still a big ordeal to overcome the effects of the abuse; and, through it all, Peggy has always been a wonderful, giving, and loving person. She has always wanted to better herself and help others, but the struggles inside of her kept her from being the person she wanted to be for a long time. Watching her suffer with depression and hospitalization was very difficult. It reminded me so much of the struggles my husband Dave went through. I watched her and her little family struggle with Peggy's constant anguish and hurt.

Peggy is a great person who tried so hard to get better. I don't know if "better" is the right word. Maybe it's more getting to a stage in life where the abuse can be put aside and not affect her in such a negative way. I have watched Peggy transform into a strong, independent woman. It's been fun watching her grow up to become a wife, mother, and a wonderful friend to so many.

I love Peggy with all my heart. She is so open to listen and understand others. As a family we have dealt with so much with mental illness and the stigma that comes with it. I love the fact that Peggy wants to take away the label of mental illness and allow all individuals the ability to be their own person. It's refreshing when I talk to Peggy and she understands how hard life really is—no excuses, no pep talks.

Sometimes things are just the way they are and we will at one point find our way. This is what Peggy has taught me. She has taught me that life is worth living but at times is hard work! She taught me that we are like an onion with lots of layers that sometimes we need to peel away to find out why we feel the way we do. She taught me that it is so important—in fact, the MOST important thing is to look to our Savior Jesus Christ to help us when all else fails. She has such a strong testimony of the atonement and how it allows all of us the ability to give our problems to the Savior. For someone who grew up hating to read, it's amazing to see her turn to her scriptures and other church materials for guidance and comfort. I love her.

Pam and me

Dear Friends!

Bottom: Me, Julie Labrum, and Amy Iverson, today

Top: Alecia Thompson Williams
Bottom: Me and Ashley Boyack

Loving Siblings

Top: Gill, Me, and Ned
Right: Me, Wendy, and Nancy

My sweet brother Dave

Link 26:

Steve's Support As a
Loving Spouse

"Hi, this is Steve. To my sweet wonderful wife who is my best friend and partner in crime: I couldn't imagine going through this life and growing old with anyone but you, Peggy. I love you with all my heart and soul."

Peggy and I have been married for 19 years and she is the most remarkable person I know. She and I have been on an incredible journey. She has always had a way with people to put them at ease and just to be able to talk with anyone. Because of her struggles and pain, she has even more compassion for those who are suffering. Her compassion has always been remarkable and she has always been a support for our close family and friends and even to strangers. Her outgoing attitude and her "realness" is what drew me to her when we were dating.

She had all of this even when she was going through a round of the doctors and hospitals and their various treatments where they all claimed to have "the answer." This was a real dark time for us both and, when I look back at it, I really don't know how we made it through. I remember a specific time when she was finally on the right road to healing that a light came on in her beautiful eyes that I love so much. It was incredible, almost too good to be true. I was afraid that it wouldn't last because there had been so many other promised solutions, but none would last. This time it was real. It wasn't a quick fix like the others had promised. It was hard work with many hours of counseling and months of struggling with why she had gone through the challenges she had and struggling with the past. Now, I can say that I have the girl I first met back and always knew was in there. There are times I worry it's going to go back, but it doesn't. I'm amazed at her drive and devotion to healing completely.

People are naturally drawn to Peggy. Sometimes I get jealous, but I appreciate so much what she has to offer and how she helps people to see the real person that they already are within. She is a true believer that we are all magnificent individuals who have so much potential. The world cries out to silence our true inner voice and medicate it for the symptom that shows itself. While medication does help, the root cause and dealing with it is the true power. Peggy can see this in others and has a real passion to help that inner voice be heard and the real and permanent healing begin. She doesn't want others to suffer as she did for so many years. Her message is a message of hope.

I'm so humbled to call Peggy my wife. I love her and love the passion she brings to my life, but I am a little biased. That's OK with me.

I was asked to share how I came about this miraculous way of being able to cope with a loved one in dire straits and still being able to survive myself. Truth is I'm not sure how, looking back. I do know this though: I had this sense of being and knowing where I came from, why I am here on the earth, and where I am going. Knowing this as the base of my understanding has helped me through many situations where things seemed so bleak. This knowledge also really helped me in understanding the true person that my wife is and who she will become once all of these mortal appendages have been removed.

I believe each one of us has a mission, and how we go about accomplishing that is between God and us. There is no right path, but you have to choose one and keep pushing along that path until you get to whatever destination it is. If the path is completed, you move to a different one, but keep trying and growing and developing. So with my sweet wife we had to keep trying different paths and keep holding onto hope that one day we would find it. We have gone down many different paths.

When we were first married I didn't believe in medication. I had this idea, not sure how it was shaped, that the medication, while it may help with symptoms, only created more problems. When Peggy told me that she had taken medication in the past but wasn't at that point, I was good with it. After about six months of marriage she started really struggling with depression. We both agreed to give the medication a try to see how it would work out. As I look back, this was when I started to see the ups and downs of this disability that she was struggling with, and this would continue until we finally got to the point where we wanted to really understand the *whys* of it.

I remember feeling that I really wanted to understand what she was going through. I was in college at this point and decided to take some psychology classes. While I learned a lot about the brain and treatments, I really didn't like one of my professors. He labeled it as a death sentence to have depression and that if you had it you should not reproduce so the gene could be stopped. This really bothered me and it kind of knocked me back a couple of steps. I knew Peggy was not that way and I knew I was not that way, having had my own battles I have fought through. It's amazing to me how closed minded some of our most educated people can be.

I started to develop a real mistrust with doctors and others who thought they knew all of the answers. We were led down many different paths, all ending in continued frustration. Every doctor promised new results, but they all started with medication, which meant changing all current ones and starting new ones all with their own side effects and withdrawals. Every once in a while, something would work great but then ultimately fail. I remember being very frustrated. I had many moments of utter despair.

The darkest moments for me were the hospitals and when she was admitted to the psych wards. I couldn't believe this was happening. It felt like our family was being torn apart. I needed to be there for my wife but I also needed to be there for my children. I didn't want them to know about what their mom was going through. I felt so alone. I didn't want anyone to know what was going on. This was my weakness I learned. We are never alone. I knew my Father in Heaven was with me. Along with that is that I had a pretty supportive family. I can only imagine what they must have been thinking. I made it clear to everyone that she would always be my wife and I would never leave her.

There was one stay that she didn't want to see me and they wouldn't let me see her. I was crushed. All I could do was hold onto my children and keep pushing along the path. Many times I didn't know where I was going; I was just going. Then came the shock treatments. I don't know of worse situations than to watch your best friend go through that. They asked me if I wanted to come into the room. My sweet father-in-law wanted to be there also; he is such a good man and example to me. Many 4 a.m. sessions we would go up to the hospital and sit with Peggy while they prepped her, put her to sleep, and then do the treatments.

After she was wheeled back to a room to recover, Dad and I would bundle up in the car to get back to her parents' house where the kids were, just in time for me to go to work. I had many patient bosses and people I worked with, along with good friends and family. I'm not sharing these things for sympathy, as I know we all have our trials that we have to go through. I really didn't want to write anything because Peggy is the one that had to go through it all. This has brought up a lot of emotions I didn't know I had inside, so I guess it's a good thing.

With all of the negative we had many wonderful experiences and had a lot of fun together. So it wasn't all bad.

When we started down this path of really healing the inner part of her, I didn't have very much hope, but I relied on her inner drive. Peggy has this amazing quality in her to know what has to be done. I sometimes have a hard time making decisions and she is the opposite. I've learned so many great qualities from her that I've tried to implement into my own life. She is the best part of me. Going through this process, I have been able to heal many parts of my past that have caused me pain.

The true miracle is when I saw Peggy after trying this new method of healing herself from the inside out. The lights were literally back on in her eyes. She has the most amazing eyes and they were so bright. I doubted at first, but the light stayed on. I couldn't believe it; I had my wife back. Now, that's not to say that there still haven't been ups and downs—there always are, that's part of life—but the deep ups and downs were healed.

I don't really like the question of "How did I cope with her disability?" because I don't see her that way, and she has had to put up with a lot from me. However, if I were to say a few things that helped along this path, they would be:

- Faith
- Hope
- Patience with both your spouse and yourself
- Having a oneness with our Heavenly Father and faith in the Atonement of Jesus Christ
- Forgiveness
- Prayer

- Fasting
- Family – allowing them in to share the burden
- And above all else: knowing where we came from, why we're here, and where we are going after this life. And I would add that nothing physical in nature will rise with us in the life to come, only the spiritual and the relationships we have

Peggy is my hero. She is such a source of strength to me. I've learned to trust her and her guidance. I've been chasing her since before this life, as she came down to earth two weeks before me. I'm still chasing her.

A Healer's Insight:
We May Find Purpose in the Scar

"But he was wounded for our transgressions, he was bruised for our iniquities...with his stripes we are healed."

~Mosiah 14:5

My name is Cheri Harris and I have helped Peggy facilitate stress release. I am not a therapist, nor a psychologist. Some patients have said talk therapy can be like throwing up issues over and over: hash it out, bring it up, painful and slow. With emotional release techniques you identify the issue, release, and change the self-limiting belief to a healing perspective. You cannot change the past, but you can change your perception and how you view yourself.

The first time I saw Peggy she was wrapped up in a blanket, literally being carried by her husband. It seemed such a desperate situation, and utterly hopeless. My first thoughts were empathy for Steve, how caring and sweet he was with her in that moment and his concern for her. After time and quite a bit of work with another doctor who helped her wean off her medications, Peggy began emotional release work with me. She was in a more functional place when we began work. I feel our work was just cleaning up the leftover cobwebs.

We began first by identifying self-limiting beliefs. These issues or negative feelings are not who you really are. As children or even adults, we create self-limiting beliefs, usually fear-based. In Peggy's experience with abuse, she formed self-doubt, feelings of unworthiness, self-hatred, and feeling unlovable. No way out, it blocks our progress and we decide that is just the way we are, part of personality, become attached to this state and live with limitations, patterns that draw vital energy and sabotage our healing. The way out is awareness, to realize new creating is now possible. We have to be willing to be accountable for our choices. It is hard to take ownership of painful experiences and want to place blame.

Peggy is amazingly visual and, as she will tell you, she is an open book. When issues come to the surface, if she senses my hesitation, she always says, "Give it to me straight." She is open to seeing and changing difficult things. Sometimes it is hard and scary to look at challenges or issues, but she always says, "Bring it on," or "Let's deal with it." She changed self-limiting behaviors, released the past, and gave forgiveness to others and self. The "glass room" Peggy struggled with was feelings of unworthiness and not knowing how to reach out as a child and adult about the abuse. We worked on breaking down those barriers in order for her to communicate wisely with those around her. Her relationship with the Savior seems to be the catalyst in healing many facets in her heart. When I ask her how she sees the healing process take place, [she says] it most likely channels into His loving, open arms willing to receive her pain.

Knowing and understanding the Atonement for others but not feeling worthy of it herself has [produced] some of the most sacred moments where we stayed in quiet contemplation until she could fully connect and apply it to herself, which seemed more difficult at times for her than others. Healing and peace through the Savior have proved to mend parts of Peggy that have seemed hopeless and broken. One of the experiences I will never forget was the day after she confronted her abuser. We spent deep reflection on what might free that last wing in her tangled web. In the end again, it was the power of the Atonement to help set her free. Peggy has such faith and inspires me with her courage to come forward with her story in hope of inspiring others who are struggling, to remind them to remember their true worth, their divine nature. The Savior atones for us and feels and knows our suffering. Our most difficult challenges lead to triumphs and blessings. Peggy has and will continue to triumph and heal.

~Cheri Harris, Training APN – Applied Psycho-Neurobiology with Dr. Klinghardt

Cheri and I, September 2013, speaking at the Utah Peer Conference for mental health where we were asked to speak together on the effects of abuse and the techniques she has used to help me combat them.

Link 28:

The Perfect Link

*"But he was wounded for our transgressions, he was bruised
for our iniquities; the chastisement of our peace was upon him; and
with his stripes, we are healed."*

~Mosiah 14:5

Abuse is a fascinating creature. We tend to equate our self-worth with its poison. It may take years if not decades to link back to our true identities as children of a loving God—not the damaged piece of flesh we believe no one cares for and discards.

On a nice summer's day when I was tossing around my college dream of becoming either a motivation speaker or a counselor of some sort, I took a drive up Parley's Canyon alone. It was a Fast Sunday (which, in the LDS church, is the first Sunday of every month where the saints grow closer to the Lord by abstaining from food and drink, as Christ did for forty days). As I hit the crossroads to turn up East Canyon, almost reaching the summit of this grand, gorgeous mountain, I felt this wave of peace rush over me.

I had been silently bickering with the Lord about my self-worth. *Why would anyone want to listen to what I have to say?* I asked Him. I was still peeling back the layers upon layers of grimy film the abuse had created, and was ashamed of some of my past ways of coping with it. I was in no way the master of my emotions. I knew I would never be perfect in this lifetime. *They'll see right through me,* I said. *I am still a "work in progress." I can't preach until I have reached a place of no longer needing to be healed.*

"How am I worth it, Lord?" I pled aloud.

A gentle yet firm reply was felt in both my heart and my head: "Peggy, you are worth it because you are *my child.*"

In the brief moment it took to feel those words, my feelings of inadequacy and fear of judgment were swept away by this truth I had forgotten for a moment. I *was* worth saving, not only as an innocent child, but even now as an adult who is *still* sorting through all the rubble of the past, ugly as it can be. I recalled the counsel I had been given long ago that many snares would entangle me throughout my life, but I would be given powerful resources to call on for strength and courage.

I have a message of hope to share. I am no more special than the next person, and it is because of that that I am capable of sharing the Lord's message of hope. We are worthy of God's infinite love because we are ALL His children! We need His love *because* of what we have walked through.

The links in my life's chain are not the same as yours, and that's okay. When we are ready, the Lord will help us see, individually, the links meant for our journeys. None of us is forever trapped in a place where the Savior cannot reach us, if we but extend our arms and place our burdens upon Him. As I have shared my story, I have felt the love of my Redeemer working through me. I testify that He is very aware of us and able to apply His healing balm only when *choose* to see our trials as stepping stones to becoming who He knows we can be. His mercy is the reason I want to reach out and help others.

Though my journey now is to be brave enough to abandon my fear and share my testimony with those whose chains of freedom are still being forged, I have many more links to discover! I will never be done learning, repenting, and linking to my Master. As we read in Ether 27:12: "And if men come unto me I will show unto them their weakness. I give unto men weakness that they may be humble: and my grace is sufficient for all men that humble themselves before me, and have faith in me, then will I make weak things become strong unto them." The chains of endless trials I thought were binding or restrictive have always been for my good, making me stronger and humbling me so that I draw closer to my Savior, for He gave us our weakness to link to Him for strength and humility. If we were already perfect like Him and had reached the end of our chains, then what purpose would we have here on Earth?

It may take a lifetime to find the Peggy I dream about becoming, but I know the Savior will support me, for He is the only perfect link to the Father.

I pray you may find your links back to our Father in Heaven. Own your voice! Trust it, acknowledge the truth, and move forward—regardless of opposition from others. Be true to yourself no matter what fear stands in front of you. God will guide you in your search for peace and freedom from a painful but necessary past. He loves you and will provide for you in the very hour of your need. Trust Him, and trust yourself.

You are worth it, and that's the honest true!

Peggy Warner Ayers

The Ayers Family

Steve, Peggy, Luke, and Grace

(Picture taken by a good friend, Tera Bekker)

Acknowledgments

I have had ample help in turning my dreams into reality. I owe many thanks to Mary Jean Waddell, a family friend who helped put thousands of emails into a storyline. I appreciate her sacrifice and wisdom, and love her very much. A "thanks" is also owed to Marie Kinghorn, a newfound friend from the last year who helped fine-comb with insightful edits; Julie Halversen Tate, Julie Labrum, and Amy Iverson for giving sage wisdom needed to fill in the gaps; and to my sweet illustrator, Jenica Whale, who patiently helped me brainstorm a meaningful cover that would capture the spirit of the book's message, and so willingly drafted up many ideas. Throughout this process I gained a new friend in her!

Lastly, to sweet Mary Parkin, whom God directed me to, as I was in need of slimming down my thoughts into a smaller version for a certain audience. She can say in fewer words what it takes 50 for me! She has worked countless hours—as did Mary Jean—to come to this final point. She was a genius learning to channel her "inner Peggy," as she called it, while she translated my run-on-sentences into comprehensive thoughts. She is a gifted writer and editor whom I thank the Lord I was led to. In the hopes of crossing the finish line for what I have envisioned for this book, we have merged our voices into one.

I feel honored to have brushed shoulders with many who have been gracious enough to give me powerful insight to reach the heart of my topic. Many times I wanted to just skim the surface, yet Mary would ask me to look deeper and not just "tell" the story but to "show" it with my every emotion. This whole endeavor has transformed my vision into what it is now. God's hand was in this during even the hardest moments when I felt most alone scribing my pain into print. Thank you, all of you, for challenging me to look deeper into the truth of my heartache so that I might properly heal.

I would be very ungrateful if I did not take a few words to express my gratitude in behalf of my support team. There were many dark hours when, if I had not had the friends and family around me lifting me up, I honestly do not know if I would be here today. Yes, my Savior never left me and I could have done it with just His love, but I am grateful I had both. I have been blessed with dear, dear friends in my life from childhood to adulthood. I don't really see a distinction between friends and family. I try to love them as if they were all my family. I am so grateful for each and every one of them in my life.

To those friends with whom I may have journeyed only a short time, please know you're in my heart always. To those who make daily impressions on my life story, bless your patient hearts for listening to my *every* whim in trying to figure out this so-called life. I love my friends! I have a huge place in my heart for all those who have loved me and who I have yet to meet and welcome as new best friends. My biggest prayer is that I will not leave anyone out of my circle of friendship.

I believe my Savior knew I needed the examples of charity and tireless love that I had and still have in the midst of me to light the way. To those who helped on the adoption side, financially and emotionally, my heart cannot express how thankful I am for your support. To the friends who listened and loved me and cared when I was my most prickly and least attractive self, I express my utmost love. I do not pretend to be the perfect woman. I am far from it. I make daily and hourly mistakes and work hard to subdue my pride, but I hope each and every one of you knows how I love you perfectly in my inner-most heart even if I don't express it properly.

If I could put into words the love and appreciation I have for my parents, it still would not be enough. They have believed in me when I was the least loveable and most unbearable to live with as a teen and as an adult. I love them with all a daughter could love. They continue to be a beacon of hope in a challenging world. To extended Ayers family, thank you for a wide girth of growth as I continue to rediscover myself. I appreciate all the hours you spent tending and loving me regardless of my ability to love back in harder years. You have taught me a lot about myself and appreciate this sincerely. Mom and Dad Ayers, I love you as a second set of parents; you raised an incredible loyal, son I pray to treasure into the eternities.

Luke and Grace, you have been the reason I held on when the dark became almost unbearable. Sometimes it takes loving someone more than yourself to push through the thorny hours of despair. I feel so many times you two were sent here to teach me more than I could ever teach you. I love you both with every fiber of my being! I may not have been the Mom you needed when you were younger, and know I will continue to fall short of what you deserve but will never give up attempting to become the mom I dream of being for both of you!

I don't want to sound trite, but I truly want my husband to know he is my prince. We are both far from perfect, but I can only imagine a heaven shared with his love surrounded by our sweet children. He has seen through my walls and looked past my insecurities and lack of trust, but mostly he has accepted me at every point of this journey. Hopefully, it will continue as we strive to become even closer in this mortality of issues. I hope I can learn to love him the way he has loved me; then I will have given back a small portion of what I want to shower him with for his undying devotion to me as a caregiver and spouse—but mostly best friend. I love you, my sweetheart.

Lastly, I want my Savior Jesus Christ to know I owe Him all of me. I have had some suggest that I have a great story, but I did not need His part in it. My reply, after searching my heart, was, "Without Him, I don't have a story." Yes, I wish I had not experienced abuse, the psych wards, the shock treatments, the loss of siblings, a niece and now a father; but I believe God knew exactly what I did need to find my way back to Him again. I was a prideful youth. I thought at times I needed no one but my anger and determination to fight back. I was oh so very wrong! There is no greater power for me in the world save the Atonement and love of my Heavenly Father and Savior Jesus Christ. I am better for my journey and hope to keep faithful and endure to the end knowing there are many more obstacles that lie ahead. Hopefully, I have learned a pattern in my life of finding the silver lining, that the only true place to find peace is in keeping His commandments and learning to give my will over to Him who created me, God himself.

You all mean the world to me. Thank you for loving me in all my funny, prickly forms. You're the angels God knew I needed in my life to make it back to His loving arms after feeling yours!

~Peggy Warner Ayers

Peggy has been gracious enough to let me, her humble co-writer, take up some space on this acknowledgments page. Let me start off by saying, "Wow!" Working on this book with Peggy has been an incredible experience. I can't thank her enough for seeing *my* worth and talent, and trusting me with this precious piece of her life.

I am grateful to my family, especially my parents and my sister for supporting me in this and my personal writing endeavors. They've never told me to give up on my dreams, even when they were comparable to Mt. Everest. I love you oodles!

Though sufficient, this acknowledgment would not be complete without a shout-out to my best buddies, "The Mob." I just love you guys! Never give up, no matter how steep the climb.

~Mary Parkin

Links Connected as One

Cherished Comments from Friends

"I admire your faith and the way you open up your beautiful heart to all of us. You speak to the vulnerable and imperfect spirits we all are and I love that about you!"
~ Lindsay Astle Ashton

"I wanted to thank you for being such a strong example of bearing one another's burdens—not being afraid to share your own stories when they give strength (to you and others) and letting adversity make you better. I love having examples in my life that so clearly show a better way. I struggle, sometimes, to open up and I love seeing ways to overcome that in the way you approach life."
~ Elizabeth Vincent

"My friend and her daughter jumped at the chance to come hear Peggy talk about her journey back to being happy and having a positive attitude about life. My friend's daughter had had similar experiences with sexual abuse as a child. She had struggled for years with this. I think her seeing Peggy happy and with a great spirit helped her realize it can truly happen. She brought a picture of the Savior and displayed it while talking. It was not only a great experience but a spiritual experience as well as she cited numerous examples of how the Atonement works to help heal the wounded. It was excellent and helped us all realize by observing her that you can go on and be happy in spite of your health, mental or other problems."
~ Sharon Jackson

"Peggy, I appreciate hearing about your abuse and all your trials, but what you have is relatable to anyone. Many of us have minds that shut down and go into despair."

~ Anonymous

"Thank you, thank you, thank you for sharing your story with me. This life is a test, not the reward. I truly believe that the greater the struggle, the greater the spirit. You are one of His greatest! Just think what you have in common with all the noble and great of this world who have overcome this mortal existence. You have been refined! I am honored to be a friend of yours!

~ All my love, Lisa Lowe

"Thanks for hosting such a wonderful evening! My favorite quote of the night: "I came to the realization that I'm not that weird." I chuckled when you said that, Peggy, but really EVERY woman should have that realization! :)"

~ Darcie Boyack

"Thank you for sharing and setting the floor to open up about the very real hardships in life and inviting healing into our hearts. It's so refreshing to be around such awesome ladies. I really enjoyed everyone that was there."

~ Merry Brown Barton

"It was such an honor to hear your beautiful story of courage and love! Thanks you so much for providing a safe, respectful environment where all those that attended could feel loved and cared for."

~ Sarah Tyler Watkins

"Your story is beautiful. You are such a great speaker with great emotion. I loved your fly/web analogy. You are so brave to share your heart and many will learn to break free of their pains because of you! You are beautiful!!!"

~ Nicole Whitman

"Wow, Peggy! I am so very impressed—you have truly been through a journey of self-discovery and I admire your strength! Thank you so much for sharing this with all of us—I know there are those of us out there that really need to hear of your journey so we can jump-start ours. Very well written!"
~ Michelle Dallon

"Peggy called me several years ago to edit something she had written because I had been recommended by a relative of hers. The first time we met, I was impressed by her honest expressions of her feelings. I had taught writing, and I quickly identified her fresh creativity and her ability to interpret life in a way to give new insights to others. I feel my heart has been enlarged by having the privilege of editing her story, and I have found in her a true eternal fiend. I love her and I love her family. I am confident that anyone who reads her story will be touched at some level and be a better person because they have met Peggy."
~ Mary Jean Waddell, editor

"The first time I met Peggy, the thing that stuck out in my mind was how friendly and funny she was. She made me feel like a friend right from the beginning.

We had a falling out for several years after I married Steve's brother but miracles happen and time shifted our relationship.

After numerous excruciating experiences, Peggy finally found a physician, who weaned her off her medication and gave her other solutions. I noticed when we talked on the phone I was talking to the Peggy I had first met. She didn't just come back; she was uncovered for the first time. Peggy was fun again, but her behavior wasn't just about being funny; she was real, caring and passionate. It wasn't until later after I had given birth to my twins that I myself felt unbalanced and got a small taste of what Peggy must've felt like all those years. Albeit my taste was a crumb to Peggy's cake, but it gave me some insight into how crippling her illness was. Peggy and I bonded during this time as I saw her physician in Provo as well. We were able to discuss our feelings with each other in a productive and non-threatening way for the first time. I discovered that the real Peggy is the most caring and unselfish person I've ever met. This was a complete turn-around for Peggy. She works harder and has been more dedicated to the process of healing than anyone I've ever known. She's gone through hell and I admire her for digging her way out. It's been so fun and an honor to be Peggy's friend again. She is not just a sister-in-law to me, but the sister I have never had."

~ Laura Ayers

"One of my best friends decided I needed the opportunity to hear Peggy speak since I was wondering about what road to take in my life, and Peggy and I had been the victims of abuse. I jumped at the chance, but was also a bit nervous deep down. However, all my worries or concerns were laid to rest as soon as I was in Peggy's presence. When you are in the room with her, you know you are in the presence of someone who is strong, humble, loving, kind and more concerned for you than she is for herself. I was impressed at how relatable Peggy was and fun. I believe a sense of humor can help us through life, and make our lives a bit easier if we choose to smile, instead of wallowing in self-pity.

There is none of self-pity emanating from Peggy. She is full of confidence, love, total acceptance and charity. After her talk, it was so nice to be able to just let it all out. I live in a world where everyone around me denies what happened to me, and I have learned I have to live with that to keep the peace in my family. Peggy reminded me that it was OK to do that. However, it was nice to share what was on my mind and in my heart because not being validated kills your heart. But I know that is just the circumstances in life right now that have made things that way, and acceptance is the key in the healing. Peggy reminded me that I ought to stick with how I've been the last couple of years...not blaming or pointing a finger at anyone, totally accepting of others, and loving unconditionally, having a sense of humor, and letting go of the things I can't do anything about.

We talked afterwards, and I was so appreciative of her taking time out of her busy schedule for me. She truly wants the message to be one of love, healing and progression, and she points you to the Master Healer, Jesus Christ.

Even if you are not religious, do not hesitate to listen to her message. Peggy isn't going to be pushing religion; she is opening space for people to heal, literally. She left time at the end of her speech for others to share anything and she took a seat to sit and listen with an open heart and mind. She was very supportive of whoever spoke, and told those strengths she saw in them. To go from being the victim and becoming the victor in our own lives is quite the challenge, and Peggy has risen to it and above it. Because of her example I know that many hearts will be touched and given a place where healing can start because so many people who have been abused feel trapped.

I feel much honored to know her and know now that we are friends. This is my point of view as to what Peggy is accomplishing. She is a wonderful woman full of exactly what others need to hear. Peggy's message is an avenue for her to share in order to help others. She doesn't take the stage for herself, so to speak, but only to enable others to hear a message of how a victim can become a victor, and she wants that message to be conveyed to others so that they might do the same. This is what I have felt every time in her presence. I hope that you will allow her message to sink into your hearts if you are someone who needs healing and doesn't know where to look. This is how I see her affecting others, striving to let them find their path back to confidence and healing and having a very beautiful life. Love you, Peggy, and thank you!"

~ Anonymous

Warner family photo in front of my childhood home, a year before we moved my parents into the home where we live now. Our family has grown since then, but this is our last photo with Dad/Grandpa Warner! Precious moment.

Ayers family photo taken together in Murray Park some six years ago. Many more family members have been added to the Ayers nest!

Above: Amazing ladies on the Warner side of the family who have impacted my life. Thank you for believing in me!

Thanks to all my supportive friends!